Dinner Music
in a
Combat Zone

ISBN 978-1-954095-26-7 (Paperback)
Dinner Music in a Combat Zone
Copyright © 2021 Jeremy Paul Ämick

For permission requests, write to the publisher at the address below.

Yorkshire Publishing
1425 E 41st Pl
Tulsa, OK 74105
www.YorkshirePublishing.com
918.394.2665

Printed in the USA

Dinner Music
in a
Combat Zone

Jeremy Paul Ämick

TULSA

CONTENTS

Acknowledgements...vii

Dedication ix

Introduction...xi

Chapter 1:   Raising an Educator 1

Chapter 2:   Building a Soldier..22

Chapter 3:   Qui Nhon, Vietnam.......................................45

Chapter 4:   Parties and Casualties 73

Chapter 5:   Unleashing the Storm..................................100

Chapter 6:   Shadows of War Lengthen 134

Chapter 7:   The Intensity of War 154

Chapter 8:   A Lingering War….......................................176

Chapter 9:   Closer to Home..195

Chapter 10: Life as an Educator......................................217

Epilogue...245

Appendix A..253

Appendix B 255

Appendix C...257

Appendix D 259

Works Cited...261

Index..269

ACKNOWLEDGEMENTS

There were several wonderful people who stepped forward during the initial stages of this endeavor, graciously relating stories and anecdotes of their memories of Roger Dean Buchta. Many shared affectionate reflections on the lessons they learned from this quiet scholar during German, history, and social science classes in high school, while others spoke with a fondness of his inimitable personality. Additionally, some warmly shared stories about the adoration he possessed for the animal kingdom—most notably his canine friends. I cannot extend enough gratitude to his brother, Don Buchta, whose assistance has been invaluable. His support afforded me the opportunity to help perpetuate the memory of a man whose life was not only significantly impacted by his service in the Vietnam War but who chose not to permit the atrocities he witnessed there to define his perspective in later years. Thank you, Don, for all you have done to help transform an idea into this biography. Finally, I would be remiss if I failed to recognize my friend, Coast Guard veteran, and superb editor, Dennis Hall, for all of the time he invested in correcting errors that weaseled their way into the manuscript.

DEDICATION

To the memory of Roger Buchta, whose quiet presence had a thunderous impact in the lives of many... both students and friends. Du wirst sehr vermisst, mein Freund.

INTRODUCTION

My first introduction to Roger Buchta came in 1990 when I entered my freshman year of high school. Sometime during that fall, I experienced my first class with the high school teacher, having already heard stories from older students noting his quiet nature and unique personality. Since Roger didn't meet the mark as an outgoing and boisterous individual, unlike many other teachers at the Russellville High School, some students chose to construct disparaging rumors about the educator's past and uncommon interests.

What most failed to realize at the time, including me to some extent, were the atrocities Buchta had witnessed while serving in Vietnam nearly a quarter-century earlier. There were times, usually within the lectures he composed for our world and American history courses, when he would make random mention of his time spent in the U.S. Army. In these moments he would occasionally share slides depicting scenes from his deployment. But we were distracted youth, generally not interested in investing any effort in comprehending the events which led to the emotional composite of the elder who taught our class; rather, we became more attuned to achieving passing grades in our various courses and participating in the next exciting and fun activity with our friends.

Despite the selfishness that defines many youths, there were those of us who grew to appreciate Buchta's inimitable personality in addition to his zest for history and the German culture. Most of us came to realize there was an undercurrent of trauma that helped shape his personality; however, we also recognized the depth of intellect we could only aspire to attain. Yet our high school days continued to pass us by while the days wore into weeks, months, and then years. Soon our class was graduating, and we all went in our separate directions.

I had the privilege of serving in the military for several years. After receiving my discharge in 2004, I reconnected with Roger Buchta while also becoming good friends with his older brother, Don. We all shared a penchant for history, and I was honored to occasionally receive invitations from the two to join them when visiting sites of local historical interest. I chronicled many of these excursions in newspaper articles I penned for the *Jefferson City News Tribune*. Other times, we would all get together for barbecues and Oktoberfest celebrations. On one memorable occasion, the three of us visited a local cemetery located deep within the forest, so that we could measure a massive oak tree that Roger wanted to "date" based up a formula he came across on the Missouri Department of Conversation website. When Roger discovered that the tree predated the American Revolution, he excitedly shared his findings with all who would listen.

Eventually, I was able to convince a hesitant Roger to allow me to interview him regarding his service in Vietnam. Several of our shared acquaintances expressed surprise that he would concede to having a newspaper article written about him, since he rarely spoke about his service other than in fleeting reflection. However, I would come to understand that there was much sadness in his story that he chose not to mention during our interview. I didn't realize most of this until after his passing.

Shortly after Roger's death, in early February 2019, Don Buchta and I became closer friends. We often held discussions about Don's departed brother. I soon discovered that Roger had written scores of letters home while in Vietnam. Many of these letters provided concise details regarding Roger's military service in addition to sharing fascinating anecdotes and keen observations. One evening, a month or so after Roger's passing, Don came by my house and dropped of the bundle of several dozen letters along with scores of photographs and slides taken by his brother during his overseas deployment. Initially, my intention was to sort through the packet and see if anything might be of interest for newspaper articles. The deeper I dug, the more convinced I became that my former German teacher's story deserved to be expanded into the format of a book.

What an utter joy it became reconnecting with friends and family of Buchta's, many of whom had been some of my teachers during my days as a student at Russellville High School. There were no ill words or sentiments uttered regarding their experiences with the late Buchta; everyone spoke of him with glowing respect and admiration. They regaled me with interesting moments from their own past interactions. Furthermore, while working on collecting some of the backstory for Roger's biography, I contacted one of the men with whom he had trained prior to his deployment to Vietnam. Prior to ending our phone conversation, the former soldier stressed to me, "Please do a good job with his book and make sure that you honor Roger for the great man he was."

It is my utmost wish that I have accomplished this daunting responsibility in at least some small measure... and that the memory of the late Roger Buchta has been perpetuated in a manner reflective of his unique and good-natured personality. This book, I sincerely hope, will also reflect Roger's dedication to providing a quality education to generations of students and highlight an individual who, though involuntarily drafted into the military, like many of his erstwhile contemporaries, went on to serve his nation without regret or complaint during the Vietnam War.

Jeremy P. Ämick
Russellville, Missouri
December 2020

CHAPTER 1

Raising an Educator

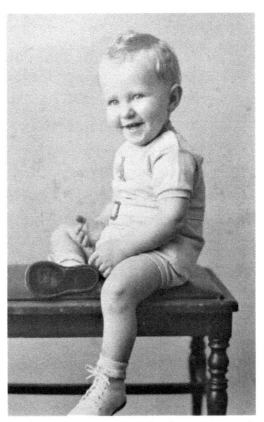

A delighted, young Roger Dean Buchta is pictured in 1946 while growing up on a farm near the rural community of Lohman, Missouri. He was the second son of William Buchta and the former Alma Koestner. Courtesy of Don Buchta

On October 28, 1944, with a number of battles unfolding throughout Europe and the Pacific, Roger Dean Buchta quietly entered the world. This was a time in which the turmoil of World War II consumed newspaper headlines in virtually every corner the globe. Born on his family's farm, near the rural community of Lohman, Missouri, the infant Buchta's inauspicious arrival was facilitated by a thirty-year-old Dr. Elbert Meredith Eberhart. Dr. Eberhart was a country physician orginally from Pennsylvania who went on to practice medicine for decades from his office in the nearby town of Russellville.[1] Dr. E.M. Eberhart served scores of families throughout the Mid-Missouri area during his many years of practice. The good doctor not only attended to the delivery of babies, but he treated patients for a variety of maladies and injuries in addition to hosting clinics to administer vaccinations for polio and other diseases.[2] In the early years of his practice, the physician was known to travel several miles to treat his patients but in later years he established an office in Russellville. Not only did he provide medical care on the local level, but Dr. Eberhart also remained actively involved in local affairs and went on to serve several terms as a member of the local school board.

Upon his entrance into the world, Roger Buchta became the second son and final child born to William and Alma Buchta, both of whom descended from German immigrants. Roger's older brother, Don, born seven years previous, remarked that payment made to the doctor for delivering his younger brother consisted of an interesting

---

[1]   The seventy-year-old Dr. E.M. Eberhart died October 24, 1984 and was laid to rest in Enloe Cemetery near Russellville, Missouri.

[2]   April 6, 1955 edition of the *Jefferson City Post-Tribune*.

form of bartering based upon a skill that had been patiently refined by their father.

"Our father had earned the reputation of producing really good wine, and when Dr. Eberhart delivered Roger our father paid him with a fifth of wine," Don Buchta chuckled. "I was only a little fella when Roger was born, and maybe dad paid him some money somewhere down the line, but if he did I never knew about it." With a wide grin, he added, "Roger always joked that all he was ever worth was a fifth of wine!" `

Don went on to explain that his younger brother built upon an early interest in becoming fluent in the German language because their mother often chose to communicate in the dialect of her forefathers when peforming tasks around the household during their childhood.

"Our grandfather, John Jacob Buchta, was an interesting character and actually came over to the United States from Germany on two separate occasions... as odd as that sounds," Don explained. "I was told that the first time my grandfather visited the United States, he was only fifteen years old and stayed awhile before returning to Germany. Then," he continued, "he came back to the U.S. and made a fortune after he purchased, and later sold, an orange grove near Los Angeles. After he sold the grove, he decided to move to the Lohman area, since he had family living there and then purchased two farms. One of these farms is where Roger and I grew up years later."

According to the September 14, 1938 edition of the *Jefferson City Post-Tribune*, prior to his death, John Buchta remained an active participant in local politics and "was engaged in cattle raising and farming." He also became "one of the pioneers in the farm organization movement... [serving] on the board of directors of the Cole

County Farm Bureau." Additionally, he was known as a man of faith and remained a dedicated member of the congregation of Trinity Lutheran Church in Russellville.[3]

Buchta's parents and many of his relatives were members of St. Paul's Lutheran Church in Lohman. Roger Buchta was confirmed in the church and remained a member of the congregation his entire life.

Don Buchta shared more details about his grandfather, who he described as a "hard SOB… physically." Although he was only two years old when his grandfather passed from a massive heart attack, Don recalls stories about the "mountain of a man" who was reputed to have possessed a near-legendary strength. Once, while breaking a horse, Jacob Buchta purportedly grabbed the mount around its beastly neck and "brought him down to the ground." Not only did their grandfather earn a reputation for being outrageously strong, but he was recognized as honest in both his professional and personal dealings.

Eventually, William Buchta, father of Roger and Don, purchased the farm from his father. In the years that followed, William and his wife raised their sons in an environment where the boys

---

3   Born in Germany on June 19, 1867, the seventy-one-year-old John Jacob Buchta passed away on September 13, 1938. He was laid to rest in the cemetery of Trinity Lutheran Church near Russellville. His wife, the former Lena Schubert, passed away in 1965 and is buried next to her husband.

engaged in hard work while at the same time, learning to embrace the outdoors. As they grew older, both the young men assisted their mother in raising and caring for her large garden. They expended countless gallons of sweat alongside their father when engaged in such laborious tasks as loading fresh-cut hay on wagons to be stored away in the barns and later used to feed their cattle. In the moments that they had free time away from their chores, the boys often enjoyed walking to the nearby Moreau River and fishing, canoeing, and engaging in other water-oriented activities. On other occasions, the brothers toted their .22 caliber rifle into the woods and fields surrounding their home to hunt rabbits and squirrels—an activity that Roger Buchta decided to give up following his return from service in Vietnam many years later.

Their upbringing also provided another link to their German heritage and traditions through their attendance at local church services. The family remained members of the St. Paul's Evangelical Lutheran Church in Lohman, which, in years past, had conducted their worship services in the German language, before making the transition to English in the years following the end of World War I. The shift from German to English "took approximately 25 years and... it was not until the

Roger Buchta is pictured as a toddler in the early weeks of 1947, when accompanying his mother, Alma, on their way to church services.

1940s that services were conducted entirely in English."[4] The church was organized in 1852 and later erected a stone church on a hill overlooking the community of Lohman. The original church building was demolished in early 1924, at which time a new church building was erected. This new church was dedicated several months later.

In 1942, two years prior to Buchta's birth, construction was finished on the new building where Roger Buchta would years later attend elementary school. As noted in the sesquicentennial book for Russeville printed in 1988, "The high school occupied the west side, and the elementary met on the east side with the gymansium in between. The cafeteria was in the basement." Additionally, in the years prior to his entering the elementary school, there was a consolidation of several outlying school districts—many of which consisted of one-room schoolhouses—that were eventually organized into the district recognized as Cole R-1. Even with the the consolidation of education buildings that resulted in classes for all twelve grades being held within a single school structure, the student body comprised less than three hundred students in the early 1950s. Virtually all students knew everyone who attended the school, regardless of their specfic grade. However, shortly after Roger began elementary school, the student body had grown to the extent that "two wings were added to the south end of the building—four elementary classrooms on the east side and a large kitchen and dining room area plus a music room on the west," all of which would have been used by a young Buchta during his days in attendance.[5]

---

[4] July 30, 1977 edition of the *Daily Capital News.*
[5] Raithel, *Russellville, Mo. Sesquicentennial: 1838-1988*, 97.

By the time Roger reached six years of age, the local school system had also grown to the extent that it became necessary to operate a network of five new buses. One of these buses would pick Buchta, and several of the neighboring children, up in the Lohman area and bring them to their elementary classes in nearby Russellville.[6] Marvin Heidbreder, whose family moved into a farm neighboring the Buctha's in 1950, explained that the bus that brought them to school was often so full of children, there was only standing room by the time it came to pick them up since they lived toward the end of the route.

"If I recall correctly, there was about twenty-seven of us in our class, and we started school at the first grade—there was no kindergarten back then," said Heidbreder. "Back in those early days, times were pretty lean for us, and since the school lunch was fifteen cents, my mom would pack our lunch because it was cheaper for her to do so."

Spending all twelve years of their schooling together, and in the same grade, Heidbreder recalls a few basic details regarding the sublte personality of his former neighbor.

"Roger was also a very quiet one, kind of stayed to himself most of the time and was on the high side of average in his classes. He always enjoyed the outdoors but never was an athletic one that was invovled in sports or anything like that," he added. "I can remember going down to one of the ponds on their place and fishing a few times, but we never did really play or run around together. My father died when I was twelve years old, so I kind of helped take over the farm and was working all of the time."

When discussing the interest Buchta later developed in the German language and history, Heidbreder added: "While we were

---

[6] March 11, 1951 edition of the *Sunday News and Tribune*.

growing up, most of the people in this area were of German descent and still spoke the language. We had the party line telephone system at our homes, and a lot of the local women would be on their telephones speaking in German."[7] Smiling, he added, "For many of us, if our parents didn't want us to know what it was they were discussing, they would speak in German."

Don explained that whenever Roger was not involved in finishing his chores around their home, or engaged in various activities outdoors, he could be found inside the house reading and writing. He enjoyed books and articles related to both world and German history.

Buchta is pictured as a sophomore in a class photograph taken while he was attending high school in Russellville, Missouri in 1960.

"He was very studious and became a great student during his elementary and high school years," said Don. "To be honest with you, nothing much about him really stands out from his early years, because he was really never involved in a lot of exciting things during that time in his life." Don further noted, "Even though he had the reputation of often being quiet and reserved in public, he was really quite talkative at home and around his close friends."

---

[7] Many rural communities once had party lines for their phone service, which meant they were part of a telephone circuit used by several customers. For instance, a telephone subscriber could pick up the phone and listen in on the conversations between other telephone subscribers in their local network.

There are many fond memories that Jane Jones, three years younger than Roger, retains of growing up in the company of her first cousin. Her father, Rudolph Koestner, was brother to the Buchta boys' mother, Alma, and the families lived on nearby farms. The extended clan frequently spent time together involved in an assortment memorable activities.[8]

"I can remember being around both Don and Roger once or twice a week back when we were kids," said Jones. "Our grandfather, Frederick Koestner, settled in the Lohman area. Our families were very close, and we would all get together on Sundays for dinner... it was just how we did things back then."[9]

As Jones went on to explain, during a number of these gatherings, Roger demonstrated at a young age his tendency toward being a social recluse. He would often leave the area where others were congregating—which might often consist of a crowd of "fifteen aunts and uncles"—to go on a walk; other times he might be found sitting under a tree off in the distance reading a book or listening and absorbing the cacophony of sounds provided by nature.

"Grandpa Koestner was a very religious man and all of us kids were always around our grandparents," Jones said. "We were taught to respect, honor, and listen to our elders." She added, "Grandpa Koestner not only farmed but he also maintained orchards and beehives, so that he could sell the honey and fruit. All of us grandkids

---

[8] The seventy-year-old Rudolph W. Koestner passed away in 1984 and is interred in Enloe Cemetery near Russellville. His wife, the former Marcella Scrivner, passed away in 2013 when ninety-one years of age and lies next to her husband. FindAGrave, *Rudolph W. Koestner*, www.findagrave.com.

[9] John Frederick Koestner had attained ninety-one-years of age when he passed away on June 29, 1961. He was laid to rest in the cemetery of St. Paul's Lutheran Church in his native community of Lohman, Missouri.

would help pick apples from the orchard, and the ones he couldn't sell because they were too bruised or had spots on them, well, we sliced up to make apple cider."

Roger Buchta, standing, third from left, participated in the Publications Class at Russellville High School during his senior year. The group afforded him the opportunity to explore his interest in writing and, as an introvert, appears to be the only school-sanctioned group in which he chose to participate. *Courtesy of Don Buchta*

On their grandfather's farm, mechanization had yet to arrive, which would have made the daily routines and agricultural tasks much easier; instead, the plows and other implements, in addition to their hay wagons, were drawn with horses. The young Roger and Don Buchta were often brought to their grandfather's house to assist with the work, usually in the company of several of their cousins.

Reiterating the role the church played in the life of Roger Buchta and his sundry cousins, Jones further explained, "We all were part of the congregation at St. Paul's Lutheran Church and were in Bible school and Confirmation classes together."

When he was younger, Jones recalls Roger participating in the organization known as "Luther League," which allowed young church members who had not yet reached confirmation age to enjoy entertaining events to help maintain their interest in the church, such as gathering to play various games or traveling to nearby Jefferson City to enjoy roller skating.

Jones added, "Again, Roger was always very quiet and was never the type to start any trouble with anyone, but he was also very intelligent. He wasn't the valedictorian of his high school class, but I believe he could easily have been." With a grin, she added, "He was so withdrawn that I don't think he wanted to be valedictorian because that would have meant he'd have to get up in front of the school at times to speak."

There was certainly good reason for many children to be silent—if not partially out of fear—during the growing tensions of the Cold War. Three weeks prior to Buchta's thirteenth birthday, the Soviet Union launched the satellite *Sputnik* on October 4, 1957. Though lacking in the technological complexities that defines many of today's satellites, the simplistic beeping of the Soviet creation struck fear across the United States. It was seen to demonstrate that a dangerous foreign nation was quickly working to develop and refine a device that could effectively deliver a nuclear strike.

Teachers were discussing the matter with their students at school, while parents were learning about the terrifying developments in Soviet armament capabilities in newspapers and through evening radio programs. This event consumed conversations wherever a person might travel, since many Americans believed their beloved country was falling behind in the technology and arms race. What resulted from these tensions; however, was the impetus for the United States to "enact reforms in science and engineering education, so that the nation could regain technological ground it appeared to have lost to its Soviet rival." Many of the educational reforms that developed in the 1950s "were spurred by investment from the National Science Foundation" and established changes in both the focus of teaching and structure of educational content that would have some manner of influence on a young and impressionable Buchta, who was attending classes at Russellville, and perhaps play a role in inspiring his later desire to become an educator.[10]

Despite any fears stirred by Soviet technological advances, life for many children continued relatively unchanged. It was during this timeframe that a thirteen-year-old Buchta demonstrated a "temporary" interest in organized sports. He participated in—perhaps through the encouragement of his parents—a summer baseball league in Jefferson City in 1958. Two hundred sixty-five boys in the age bracket of twelve to fourteen years old from around Mid-Missouri made up thirteen intermediate baseball teams that played

Frances Engelbrecht first met Roger Buchta in 1959, when she taught his sophomore English class at Russellville High School. Years later, she and Roger would serve together as teachers at the high school.

---

[10] Powell, *How Sputnik Changed U.S. Education*, www.news.harvard.edu.

an average of twelve regular games that summer. Many fraternal organizations and businesses, such as Mutual of Omaha, a local grocery store, and the Veterans of Foreign Wars sponsored teams with Buchta playing for the local Eagles Club.[11] As Don Buchta recalled of his younger brother, "I can vaguely recall him playing ball, and I remember that he got quite a few hits but, then for some reason, he decided that he didn't want to do that anymore."

Frances Renken grew up several miles from the Buchta family near the small community of Enon and graduated from Russellville High School in 1954. She attended Central Missouri State College (now University of Central Missouri) in Warrensburg, graduating with a bachelor's degree in education in 1958. She went on to teach English classes at Tipton High School during the 1958-1959 school year and, a few weeks after finishing her first teaching year, married Curtis Engelbrecht at Olean Christian Church.[12] Mrs. Engelbrecht was soon hired by the Russellville School District and, in the fall of 1959, began teaching language arts/English classes in addition to "Publications," which included compiling the yearbook and weekly newsletter that was printed in local newspapers.[13]

"I had Roger in my sophomore English class," recalled Frances Engelbrecht. "Those early classes of a young teacher's career often remain clear in your memory because you are just getting started and everything is new." She continued, "I would seat students in my

---

[11] May 15, 1958 edition of the *Jefferson City Post-Tribune*.
[12] The sixty-seven-year-old Curtis Paul Engelbrecht passed away on July 15, 2004, and is interred in Eugene Cemetery in rural Cole County, Missouri. He was drafted into the U.S. Army in the early 1960s, serving two years in the early days of the Cold War.
[13] June 20, 1959, edition of the *Daily Capital News*.

classes in order of their last names to help me learn their names and I can remember Roger sat over by the windows of the classroom. He was very intelligent but quiet, never raising his hand when questions were asked."

Buchta and Engelbrecht had the privilege of serving together for many years as colleagues and educators at Russellville High School, becoming two of the most venerated teachers among the students.

The yearbook for the Russellville High School, called *War Whoop* in recognition of the school's Native American mascot, helps confirm many of the recollections of former friends and classmates indicated that Buchta was often reserved and could fade into the background. Aside from noting his senior-year membership in the Publications Class —the group that produced periodic school newsletters and the annual yearbook—there is no indication that he chose to participate in any of the other school-sanctioned groups or extracurricular activities. The Publications Class appeared to offer him an outlet to explore and refine his talent for writing, which he would continue to discreetly develop in the ensuing decades.

"I think that Roger really enjoyed the Publications Class because it required a lot of organizational skills," said Miriam Bond, a former classmate of Buchta's who was also a member of the aforementioned class. "I enjoyed having him in my classes and he was always willing to help anybody with their studies." She added, "He was very repectful of others and always polite, but he kind of did his own thing, kept to himself and didn't pal around with anyone that I remember."

The summer of 1961, days prior to Buchta beginning his senior year of high school at Russellville, delivered a historic event that not only helped inspire his development as a budding German historian, but also became one of the most iconic moments of the Cold War—

the erection of the Berlin Wall. In 1945, the year following Buchta's birth, Germany became a fractured country that was divided into four occupational zones. The United States occupied the south, France the southwest, Great Britain the northwest and the Soviet Union—who had allied with the U.S. during the war—taking control of East Germany. Berlin, as the capital city, was likewise sectioned into four occupational zones. The relationship between the United States and the Soviet Union became fractured to such an extent after World War II that the two countries soon became engaged in an arms development race.

The Berlin Wall was born as a result of these unyielding tensions with the Soviet Union. Construction began in August 1961 in an effort "to stop an exodus from the eastern, communist part of divided Germany to the more prosperous west." The Soviet Union became alarmed by the continuing loss of population from the areas they controlled in the east. Estimates indicate that "[b]etween 1949 and 1961 more than 2.6 million East Germans, out of a total population of 17 million, had escaped."[14] What began as simple barrier of barbwire and bricks to separate the Soviet-controlled sectors from the democratic western sectors soon evolved into a "six-foot-high [later raised to ten feet], 96-mile-long wall of concrete blocks, complete with guard towers, machine gun posts and searchlights." This barrier would sordidly define much of the world's perception of the German landscape for the next three decades.[15]

Several years later, the Berlin Wall became a focal point of interest in Roger's discussions during the world history classes he instructed

---

[14] Connolly, *Whatever Happened to the Berlin Wall?*, www.theguardian.com.
[15] History Channel, *Berlin is Divided*, www.history.com

at the high school level. Roger would become visibly animated when explaining the background, origins, and impact of the Cold War to his students. He personally continued to expand his knowledge and interest in the social, political, and economic details of Germany as the years passed. This interest provided Roger with a enduring connection to the country that was his grandfather's homeland.

A slender, seventeen-year-old Roger Buchta graduated from Russellville High School in 1962 and entered classes at Lincoln University several weeks later.

These historic events notwithstanding, Don Buctha went on to explain that during his younger brother's high school years, there was a local girl from the nearby community of Centertown that he dated on occasion, but the relationship never developed into anything more serious than a close friendship. When Roger was approaching his graduation from Russellville High School in the spring of 1962, any romantic interests he may have previously maintained seemed to evapoarate. Roger made the decision to become an educator, setting his sights on attending a local university to receive the education that would help transition his dream into a reality.

Beginning his courses at Lincoln University in Jefferson City in the fall of 1962, Roger witnessed yet another iconic moment of the Cold War. This disturbing event was a fold of history when many Americans believed they would fall victim to a nuclear attack. This event became known as the Cuban Missile Crisis. Evolving over a period of less than two weeks, this event was a "direct and dangerous confrontation between the United States and the Soviet Union during the Cold War and was the moment when the two superpowers came closest to nuclear conflict."[16] The height of tensions came when Cuban premier, Fidel Castro, agreed to allow the Soviet Union to place nuclear missiles in Cuba with the intention of preventing an invasion from the United States, who he recognized as an enemy. This was considered a pressing and immediate threat, since it would mean the Soviets would possess a nuclear arsenal located ninety miles from the mainland of the United States and could, with relative ease, launch a deadly strike against such high-profile targets as New York and Dallas. On October 22, 1962, President John F. Kennedy went on television to share with the nation some of the details that existed with regard to the growing tensions. At this time, he also announced the implementation of a naval blockade intended to prevent delivery of any additional nuclear missiles to Cuba. What many believed would assuredly result in the mutually-assured destruction of both superpowers during this stressed period ended with a resolution. It was agreed that the Soviet Union would dismantle their nuclear sites in Cuba while the United States would lift the blockade around the island country and remove all of their Jupiter missiles from Turkey by April 1963.

These historic Cold War events likely provided much fodder for fascinating and engaging discussions in several of Buchta's college courses. As the semesters rolled by at Lincoln University, when he was not busy studying, Roger worked a part-time job. He would

---

[16] Department of State, *The Cuban Missile Crisis*, <u>https://history.state.gov</u>.

occasionally receive some financial assistance towards his education from his father.

Founded in 1866 by newly-freed slaves who has served as soldiers with the 62nd and 65th United States Colored Infantry Regiments, the legacy of what began as Lincoln Institute grew exponentially in the years after the Civil War. Lincoln Institute became a land-grant college in 1890, and through legislative action in 1921 was renamed Lincoln University. Though initially founded to serve the educational needs of African American students, in September 1954, "following the attorney general's ruling on the Supreme Court decision regarding segregation in public-supported educational institutions, Lincoln University opened its doors to all qualified applicants."[17]

Childhood neighbor and classmate, Marvin Heidbreder explained, "I believe Roger was one of only three men from our high school class who went on to get college degrees and then become a teacher. Back then, most everyone just went to work and hardly anyone went off to college. If I recall correctly, I was told that Roger was able to get his degree for somewhere around eight hundred dollars— two-hundred dollars a year—which is something you sure couldn't do these days."

The *Sprinfield News-Leader* reported on December 7, 1962, approximately four months after Buchta began his classes at Lincoln University, that "state schools do not charge Missouri residents tuition but have a fee system… (of) $175 to $200 at the state colleges" for each enrollment year.[18]

---

[17] Goodwin, *Official Manual State of Missouri 1965-1966,* 589
[18] December 7, 1962 edition of the *Springfield News-Leader.*

The end of his freshman year was also an interesting period for Buchta to be attending Lincoln University. Students and facutly at the historically Black educational institution observed the landmark passage of the Civil Rights Act of 1964, which was signed into law by President Lyndon Johnson on July 2, 1964. Growing up in a rural, agrarian community and attending elementary and high schools, that at the time had no African American students, Roger's educational experiences at Lincoln became the first time he learned and studied in a diverse environment. Touted as the "nation's premier civil rights legislation, the Civil Rights Act "outlawed discrimination on the basis of race, color, religion, sex, or national origin, required equal access to public places and employment, and enforced desegregation of schools and the right to vote."[19] Prior to the Act's passage, there had been boycott's, protests, and other significant events that took place as part of the Civil Rights Movement. When Buchta returned to classes as a junior in September 1964, the passage of the Act, and its subsequent implementation, served as the basis for many thought-provoking discussions not only within their classes, but among members of the student body outside of their classes. Sadly, the Act would not ensure equal rights whether in reality or perception as five years later, Lincoln University became ground zero for student protests and civil disorder over the Vietnam War and civil rights infringements. These protests resulted in a fire that gutted the student union and led the governor to send in state troopers and call up Missouri National Guard troops to quell the disturbance.[20]

---

[19] National Park Service, *Civil Rights Act of 1964*, www.nps.gov.
[20] December 16, 1999 edition of the *Washington Post*.

Classes and part-time work were for Buchta supplemented by an introductory level of military training required of all males attending Lincoln University. Military training on the campuses of institutions of higher learning in the U.S. had an extensive legacy dating back to the American Revolution. However, it was a "concept [that] expanded dramatically when President Abraham Lincoln signed the Morrill Act in 1862," which granted the states "acres of public land to establish institutions of scientific learning," while also requiring that they establish programs of military instruction.[21] The Reserve Officer Training Corps (ROTC) program grew and expanded during both World War I and World War II and became a compulsory program for men during the first two years they attended a state college or university. However, during the 1960s, the unpopularity of the Vietnam War and the military draft caused the administration at many educational institutions to become disenfranchised with the concept of mandatory military training. As a result, many ROTC programs underwent the transition from compulsory to voluntary during this period. Others were altogether dissolved.

In the years following Buchta's graduation, the ROTC program at Lincoln University eventually transitioned to a voluntary program. However, this program continues to see high levels of student enrollment. These two years of compulsory military instruction served as Buchta's introduction to the structure of the U.S. Army, which would provide a baseline of experiences he could later draw upon when receiving his own call to the colors and entry into active duty service.

---

[21] Wissing, *The Return of ROTC*, www.legion.org.

Upon his graduation in the spring 1966, Buchta was presented his bachelor's degree in social science and a minor in German. Roger also earned his certification to teach at the elementary and secondary level at the same time. Since he was no longer enrolled in school, Roger realized that it was only a matter of time before he would be drafted into the military, since U.S. invovlement in the Vietnam War continued to escalate. In the weeks that followed, Roger watched as scores of his friends and acquaintances, many of whom were his own age, received their draft notices and were subsequently inducted into the armed forces. His suspicions proved correct when, only a few months after graduating from college, Roger's draft notice finally arrived in the mail and suspended any plans he may have developed for pursuing a career in teaching. His focus now became making preparations to leave home and complete whatever training was required by the U.S. Army, saying his goodbyes to his family, and embarking upon his own military adventure.

CHAPTER 2

Building a Soldier

Following his induction into the U.S. Army, Roger Buchta trained as a medic at Ft. Sam Houston, Texas, prior to receiving assignment to an ambulance platoon with Company A, 47th Medical Battalion at Ft. Hood, Texas. The battalion was at the time attached to the 1st Armored Division, whose patch is pictured.

The year 1966 would become one of the busiest of times for the Selective Service System during the Vietnam War. This period of time saw the greatest number of young men drafted into military service. During this year alone, a staggering total of 382,010 young bodies were compelled into the military, including the recently graduated Buchta. In the years that followed, the number of men drafted into the military in the United States would drop exponentially.[22] Estimates reveal that, despite popular belief, only twenty-five percent of the men serving within the U.S. military in combat zones during the Vietnam War were draftees. Because of the system of conscription in place at the time, many young American men chose to volunteer for the armed forces in order to have a greater choice over which division in the military, which branch of service, and, perhaps, which military occupational specialty they would be assigned. Despite his suspicions that the draft would eventually snag him as it had scores of others, Buchta chose to wait. Being drafted would provide Roger with a two-year commitment rather than forcing him to fulfill either a three or four-year term of service if he instead chose to enlist.

"Everybody was going (to war) back then; there were so many being drafted," said Roger Buchta during a 2014 interview, describing his reaction upon the receipt of his draft letter. "It was something that I just expected to happen."

In the latter weeks of 1966, Buchta was sent to Fort Hood, Texas—a sprawling military base named in honor of Confederate General John Bell Hood—to embark upon the initial hurdle every draftee and recruit knows as basic combat training or "boot camp."

---

[22] Selective Service System, *Induction Statistics*, https://sss.gov.

Located in Central Texas, the Army post was established as Camp Hood during World War II and did not become a permanent U.S. Army installation until the spring of 1950. In its early years of existence, Camp Hood trained tank destroyers to fight overseas in World War II, but as the years progressed it became known as Fort Hood, and it took on a basic training component in its overall mission structure. Currently, the fort extends across approximately 215,000 rugged—yet flat—acres and remains the largest active-duty base for the U.S. military.

The training mission to prepare troops for potential service in the growing conflict in Southeast Asia began to build in 1965, at which time the post "began receiving recruits and inductees for basic combat training…" Additionally, during this period, Fort Hood underwent "millions of dollars in construction" that helped make the post's "facilities compatible with a permanent Army post."[23] Many of these improvements included the construction of new facilities such as the Darnall Army Community Hospital, where Buchta would in the coming months receive some of his medical experience and training.

In the weeks prior to his arrival at Fort Hood, a local incident quickly exploded onto the national news scene that was motivated by a group of soldiers who were coined the "Fort Hood Three." The scandal unfolded in June 1966, when three soldiers stationed at Fort Hood refused orders for deployment to Vietnam on the grounds that they "could not in good conscience take part in an illegal, immoral, and unjust war of aggression." The attorney who represented the

---

[23] Greater Killeen Chamber of Commerce, *History of Fort Hood*, www.killeen-chamber.com.

three soldiers attempted to have the civil liberties case heard before the Supreme Court, but it was refused on the grounds "that the issue is political rather than legal."[24] For refusing orders for service in Vietnam, the three soldiers were "imprisoned for the remainder of their service [in the United States Disciplinary Barracks] at Fort Leavenworth in Kansas."[25]

The legal proceedings did not hinder the U.S. Army's processing of new recruits, and young men continued to pour onto the fort to begin their cycle of training. Upon his arrival at the Induction Center at Ft. Hood, Buchta would have received the gruff welcome extended to all prospective soldiers. He would have had his hair buzzed from his scalp by a barber wielding a pair of clippers. This ritual would be followed by standing in line to receive his first issue of soldier's clothing. Roger would also have endured countless injections from medical staff who administered a variety of immunizations. Shortly after his arrival, Roger, and his fellow recruits, also completed a written aptitude test. This test was intended to

Buchta took this photograph of fellow soldier and medic Alan Hall in early 1967, while the two were serving together at Ft. Sam Houston. Both Buchta and Hall were scheduled to deploy to Vietnam in the same timeframe.

---

[24] July 19, 1970 edition of the *Bridgeport Post*.
[25] December 12, 2019 edition of the *Herald-News*.

help assess a soldier's competencies for placement in a particular military career field (Military Occupational Specialty, otherwise known as "MOS") following the completion of their boot camp. The next eight weeks were full of physical activities designed to condition the raw recruits and were endured under a variety of strenuous environments. To this end, the recruits spent time running, maneuvering obstacle courses, and crawling under barbed wire while machine-gun rounds screamed by only inches above their heads. During their initial training, Buchta and the raw recruits also spent time engaged in field exercises, where the received an introduction to basic military maneuvers and map reading. Additionally, as noted on Buchta's discharge document, he gained familiarization with the M-14 rifle, qualifying as a marksman with the weapon. It was not long thereafter that the M-14 was phased out of service, and the newer M-16 rifle became the rifle of the Vietnam War era.[26]

While Roger underwent his basic training and completed the transformation from civilian to soldier, someone situated in decision-making levels well above the young private's paygrade selected the specific military occupation deemed best suited for Buchta. Roger soon learned that he would attend advanced training to serve in the position commonly referred to as "combat medic." This decision was made despite Roger's having no previous medical background. Roger once jokingly remarked, "The only medical training I ever received was delivering calves, kittens, and puppies once in a while on the farm when I was growing up."

In early weeks of 1967, Buchta graduated from basic combat training. Years later, he would remark to his older brother that he

---

[26] Feng, *M-14 Rifle*, www.armyhistory.org.

was "surprised" by how easy his basic training had actually been. Whether this was due to his exceptional physical condition at the time or a training regimen that had become expedited and lax, the young soldier believed boot camp would be a greater challenge. One aspect of the training cycle he did find to be rather taxing was the bayonet course, which, he later explained with a sigh of relief, only lasted one day.

Roger's next training stop came with his transfer to Fort Sam Houston, Texas. Here he received his indoctrination into military medical care in the position the U.S. Army formerly classified as a "91B"—a Medical Specialist.[27] During the ten weeks of advanced training, Roger received classes on basic anatomy, physiology, the treatment of shock, and administering an IV in addition to carrying the injured and applying tourniquets and morphine. The medical training at Fort Sam Houston also provided instruction on trauma techniques and battlefield medicine that would be used in the coming months. Many of the trainees would use these techniques to help care for soldiers wounded in combat situations, such as those that might occur in the humid and deadly jungles of South Vietnam.

Steve Dunn is a 1967 graduate of Russellville High School and earned a Silver Star for valor while serving as a medic in Vietnam. Prior to serving overseas, Steve underwent a regimen of training similar to Buchta's. His training occurred two years later, when he became a medic at Fort Sam Houston. Dunn explained, "One of the things I remember about my time in training is that they taught us how to administer shots. First, we practiced doing it on oranges, and then we

---

[27] In 2010, the U.S. Army converted the 91B Medical Specialist to the 68W Healthcare Specialist.

moved on to giving shots of saline water to some of our fellow train-ees while the instructors observed us, making sure we didn't pump them full of air." Dunn added, "We learned how to clean and ban-dage wounds and prepare a casualty for movement to a higher level of care, but there was also a physical aspect to the training because we had to learn to do the fireman carry in case we had to evacuate a casualty from an area."

With the arrival of spring came Buchta's graduation from his training as a medical specialist and his assignment to an ambulance platoon with Company A, 47th Medical Battalion under the 1st Armored Division, which was located back at his basic training site of Fort Hood. The proud lineage of the 47th Medical Battalion dates back to 1939 when it was initially constituted in the U.S. Army. The battalion served overseas during World War II and was re-designated the 47th Armored Medical Battalion by the end of the war. In later years, the battalion went through many changes, and following a period of deactivation, was reactivated as the 47th Medical Battalion at Fort Hood, Texas, in 1951.[28]

Now that the twenty-two-year-old soldier had all of his initial training requirements behind him, Roger quickly integrated into his new unit and began writing home about the preparatory exer-cises they were conducting. His letters would be prolific throughout his service in the Vietnam War. Several dozen of the writings Roger penned to his family survived the passage of decades. Sadly, only four letters exist that tell of the time he served stateside with his unit prior to his overseas service. These letters provide rich detail of the daily

---

[28] Global Security, *47th Brigade Support Battalion*, https://www.globalsecurity.org/military/agency/army47fsb.htm.

happenings in the U.S. Army. They also provide remarkable insight into the man behind the pen and his experiences of preparing for his inevitable deployment overseas.

* * *

Pvt. Roger Buchta
Company A, 47th Medical Battalion
Ft. Hood, Texas 76545
April 1, 1967

Dear Mom:

Enclosed is a little gift I bought for you for Mother's Day. I sure hope it arrives in good condition.[29]

This week we went to the field overnight. Actually, it was more like a Boy Scout camping trip than a training exercise. Everyone carried radios, snacks and other little items of comfort. Some even brought soda and beer. Those boys who were in the ambulance platoon, including myself, were fortunate enough to be able to sleep in the ambulances. The rest slept on cots. It is not safe to sleep on the ground because of scorpions and snakes. The exercise certainly helped to break the monotony of the daily routine.

---

[29] Buchta is referring to a lovely Mother's Day Card featuring a stunning park scene with a pink bow attached to the front of the card.

I am planning on coming home the last of May if my leave request is accepted. If it is not accepted, perhaps you, Don and Dad can come down. I will get a three-day pass and we will go to San Antonio. This is a city I am sure you would really enjoy.

I sure hope everyone is well and enjoying the beauty of spring as it reveals itself about this time of year. I am sure you can remember when I have made some rather critical remarks about the landscape of Central Missouri; but believe me, after living in the barren wasteland around Ft. Hood, I have developed a different opinion of Missouri. There are no wildflowers, tall trees or lush foliage which adorn the Missouri landscape here in Central Texas—only scrub oaks, cacti and dust. Of course, some people apparently like to live in an area such as this.

In closing, I hope you have a very joyous Mother's Day and also a very happy birthday. Say "hello" to everyone for me. Naturally, that includes Otis, Sissy and Bootsie. I sometimes wonder if they will remember me when they see me again. Write when you can.

Love,
Roger

* * *

As a young man, Roger had spent his early years enjoying the lush green beauty of the mid-Missouri countryside. He had on many occasions toiled in the gardens and fields rich with crops and vegetables, and his letters expose a level of homesickness brought on by his continued immersion in the dusty and desolate surroundings he lived and trained in while at Fort Hood. Furthermore, Buchta was an "animal lover," as described by his brother and close acquaintances, and being removed from his dogs while in Texas was comparable to being separated from members of the family.

Attempts at peace negotiations to end the war in Vietnam continued during his time at Fort Bragg, providing Roger and his fellow soldiers a glimmer of hope that their services would not be needed in a combat zone. These attempts at peace consisted of a Polish initiative in late 1966 that was code-named MARIGOLD; depressingly, this attempt at peace suffered an embarrassing failure. The Polish negotiations were followed by another third-party attempt by the British prime minister in early 1967, that aspired to bring all the necessary belligerents to the point of some form of resolution. However, the United States had toughened in its position and this endeavor at brokering some form of reconciliation also came to an unfortunate end.[30]

These failed attempts at reaching some form of resolution in the Vietnam War would have little direct influence on Buchta since his training continued and he came to understand that he would soon be leaving the United States for overseas service. He was not discouraged by this development. Rather, Roger accepted it for the reality it was and continued to inform his family of any new devel-

---

[30] Herring, *America's Longest War*, 167-169.

opments in his pending deployment as soon as he was made aware of them. As explained in his letter to family, dated August 19, 1967, Roger had been given much detail regarding with whom he would serve upon his arrival in Vietnam. Although this, such as is common with the military, was subject to change… just as he would soon discover. He maintained a positive outlook on his pending deployment, acknowledging that it would be an opportunity to put some money into savings through the Savings Deposit Program, which was an early indication of his inclination and interest toward saving money. This specific military saving program dates to 1966 and extended the opportunity to military members serving in a permanent duty assignment outside the United States the opportunity to deposit "unallotted current pay and allowances" up to $10,000 into a savings account with a guaranteed rate of return of ten percent.[31]

* * *

Pvt. Roger Buchta
Company A, 47th Medical Battalion, 1st Platoon
Ft. Hood, Texas 76545
August 19, 1967

Dear Mom, Dad and Don:
I suppose I better begin by relating some rather
unexpected news. I am going to Vietnam. A levy
came down this week and took five of us who had

---

[31] DOD Financial Management Regulation, *Savings Deposit Program*, 51-4.

basic and AIT together[32]—*Boice, Carman, Bailey, Hall, and myself. We are supposed to be in Nam by the first week of October. We requested a thirty-day leave which means we should start clearing next week and be home by at least September 1st. Of course, there is no assurance that we'll get thirty days but the chances are good we will.*

I am supposed to go to the 91st Medical Evacuation Hospital, which is about twenty miles from Saigon.[33] *Each of us are going to a different unit but we'll all be within a twenty-five-mile radius of each other. In fact, Hall will be in a dispensary which is in the hospital where I will be. Carman will be in an ambulance company in Saigon; Boice will be in a field hospital outside Saigon; and Bailey will be in a field hospital in Saigon. So, we should be able to come into contact with each other quite frequently, especially Hall and me. A fellow in our company who just returned from 'Nam said he was stationed where Hall and I will be. He stated the hospital where I am going is fully modern, air-conditioned and pretty safe from enemy attacks. So, that's good to know. He said the evacuation hospital is the last place where a casualty goes before, he is evacuated from Vietnam. In fact, he told me that*

---

[32] AIT is the acronym for "Advanced Individual Training," which is essentially a military career school.

[33]

periodically I would accompany casualties that are being evacuated to Korea, Japan or the states. He spoke quite highly of the place so I guess that is some consolation. Then, too, we will get overseas and combat pay. We should net well over three hundred dollars a month. We also found out that merchandise in the PXs is sold wholesale. One can even buy cars directly from the manufacturer for wholesale and free of taxes. If you buy a car in 'Nam it is waiting for you when you get home. Many guys buy cars this way. I am hoping I can buy a console stereo, tape recorder, radio combination while I am in Nam. It will be delivered at home. I should also be able to save a fairly respectable amount of money. The Army has a savings program for those in 'Nam whereby one can earn as much as 10% interest. So, financially a tour in Nam can be pretty lucrative.

I won't know any more than what I've already told you until orders come down. They should come down this week or next. We are supposed to fly to San Francisco from home. There we will get our gear. From there we fly to Hawaii and then to Nam. That's about all I know at this point. Carman, Boice, Hall and I are going to try to meet in St. Louis and leave together.

> *Saturday night I met Don Linsenbardt at the*
> *bowling alley. I had no idea he was at Ft. Hood. He*
> *said he has five months left in the service.*[34]
>
> *So that's about all for now. As soon as I get*
> *more detailed information, I'll pass it on. Say hello*
> *to everyone for me. Get the spinners ready; the cat-*
> *fish are going to catch hell. Write when you can.*
>
> *Roger*

* * *

As noted in his previous letter, Private Buchta anticipated he would be assigned to the 91st Medical Evacuation Hospital. The September 26, 1966 of the *Town Talk* (Alexandria Louisiana) explained that the soldiers at the hospital had recently finished a successful field training exercise during which "(e)verything from first aid to surgery was reenacted under simulated combat conditions." The article further detailed the structure of the hospital in a combat environment,. The journal indicated that hospitals consisted of "(f) our fully equipped hospital tents, placed in the form of a cross, (that) provided pre-operative, surgery and post-operative areas."[35] The field exercise was the culmination of an eight-week training period to

---

[34] Don E. Linsenbardt achieved the rank of Specialist 4 while serving in the U.S. Army. A native of Lohman, Linsenbardt married the former Linda Hahn on April 11, 1970. The forty-one-year-old veteran passed away September 18, 1986, and was laid to rest in Hawthorn Memorial Gardens in Jefferson City. The April 18, 1970 edition of the *Daily Capital News.*

[35] September 26, 1966 edition of the *Town Talk.*

familiarize the staff with the roles they would fulfill when deployed to Vietnam. Under normal conditions, the 91st operated as a four-hundred-bed hospital, but it could be enlarged to a six-hundred-bed capacity should the need arise.

By November 1966, noted the *Daily Register*, the 91st was in Vietnam, becoming "the first medical unit there to build its own hospital." In December 1967, the hospital was "located in Tuy Hoa, south of Quin Hon, and north of Nha Trang." The newspaper provided more details of the hospital's arrival noting that after opening its first one hundred beds on March 15, 1967, they had already begun receiving and treating both American and Vietnamese casualties of the war. Additionally, after the hospital was established and running as smoothly as could be expected under the trying and unknown circumstances of war, they constructed a small clinic near the perimeter of the hospital. Here they often treated between one and two hundred Vietnamese daily, assisting those "suffering from varying types of disease as well as general malnutrition."[36]

The next communication Buchta sent to his parents indicated there remained much speculation about when he would depart for his overseas assignment and where he would be assigned once he arrived. Regardless, his communication notes that he continued to refine his skills by training in his designated medical specialty and remained prepared for the next step in his military journey—wherever that may carry him.

* * *

---

[36] December 14, 1967 edition of the *Daily Register* (Red Bank, New Jersey).

Pvt. Roger Buchta
Company A, 47th Medical Battalion, 1st Platoon
Ft. Hood, Texas 76545
August 27, 1967

Dear Mom, Dad and Don:

I suppose the time has come to take another leave although under different circumstances than before. We have not received any definite information, but we start about three or four days of jungle training Monday (August 28), thus we should hear something this week. The chances are that we should be home the first week of September.

I don't have too much information about these few days of jungle training. Monday we are supposed to attend classes, watch movies, etc. Although we don't know anything for certain about the remainder of the training, we heard that we'll go through Vietnam Village. The post has built a Vietnamese village which is used for training purposes. The village contains everything from mines to snipers. It is supposed to be a fairly interesting exercise. One day we'll probably qualify with the M-16 and the .45. After the training, if the orders come down, we'll start clearing. This is quite an ordeal and may take a day or two. After that it is bye, bye Ft. Hood.

I've already got most of my possessions packed. The latter part of the week I'm going to start sending some of them home by mail. About three boxes will have to be sent home. All my military garb except a suit or two will be turned in here. In San Francisco we'll get special clothes. So, about all we'll have to take home is a suitcase. All I hope to have to carry home will by my TV and tennis racket. So that's about the way things stand at this point. I'll inform you as soon as I receive more definite information concerning our leave.

This last week I worked at a surgical clinic at the hospital. It was very interesting work. All I had to do was assist the doctors when they performed minor surgery. I had to prepare the patients, assist the doctors and then clean up. I also had to assist the doctor when he performed a proctoscopy (examination of the rectum). I really learned a great deal [during] the four weeks that I've been at the hospital. The acquired knowledge should come in handy in 'Nam.

That's about all I have for now. Say hello to everyone for me. Write soon.

Roger

* * *

In his letter, Buchta noted that he and many of his fellow soldiers preparing for deployment to Vietnam were introduced to anticipated combat environments that might be encountered overseas through the training site coined the "Vietnam Village" on Fort

Hood. Vietnam Village was a replica of a village similar to those the soldiers might be encounter in Vietnam, with "black-clad soldiers and civilians of unknown allegiance," reported the *Austin American-Statesman*. The newspaper further noted that, in addition to the soldiers in training who engaged in combat assaults against the mock village, the soldiers would also endure ambushes by faux Viet Cong soldiers. They were "harassed by booby traps and snipers, who after firing would disappear in a complex tunnel system under the huts."[37] The village fulfilled an important role at the post by creating a realistic exercise preparing Private Buchta and others soon to depart for service in the jungles of Southeast Asia.[38]

* * *

Pvt. Roger Buchta
Company A, 47th Medical Battalion, 1st Platoon
Ft. Hood, Texas 76545
September 5, 1967

Dear Mom, Dad and Don:
Another week has elapsed. At this writing
we have received no word about going on leave or
Vietnam. Last week we were supposed to take a

---

[37] Viet Cong were a Communist-led guerilla force that fought in support of the North Vietnamese Army during the Vietnam War. The combat tactics of the Viet Cong included the launching of surprise attacks against U.S. and South Vietnamese forces and then being able to essentially disappear into the undergrowth.

[38] July 25, 1967 edition of the *Austin American-Statesman*.

three-day training course on Nam but it was cancelled. I don't know if we will take it this week or not. Thus, I know about as much now as I did when I wrote you last, namely nothing. Maybe they will forget about us. Ha!

This last week I worked at the hospital again. This was my first week at CMS (Central Material Supply). In this area instruments are sterilized, linen folded, and surgical packs made. It is not only boring but very tiring work. But I'll only have four more days at CMS before I go on to something else, providing, of course, we don't receive any orders by then.

I got three days this weekend due to Labor Day. Saturday, I took a driving commitment for a fellow in our barracks (dispensary) who had plans of going to Houston. Since almost everyone went away for the long weekend nobody bothered me and I got a good night's sleep. I took my TV to the dispensary with me and watched "Lawrence Welk" and "Ironsides." The CQ [Charge of Quarters], or fellow in charge, had an electric guitar so we just sat around playing the guitar and watching TV. It sure was an easy way to earn $10. With the money I bought a little Kodak Instamatic camera similar to the one I brought home at Christmas. We figured it would be a good idea to take a camera with us to 'Nam. Although there is probably nothing very photogenic in the 'Nam, we're are supposed to stop in

Hawaii and Tokyo. Then, too, those serving in Nam get two weeks a year for rest and recuperation. One can go to a number of places including Honolulu, Manila, Bangkok, Australia and Tokyo. I hope to spend at least a week in Australia and Bangkok, so I may be able to get some really good pictures. Before I come back, I hope to buy a better camera. Everything you buy in Nam is ½ or less of the actual retail price.

I believe our problems regarding our trip home may be solved. Boice's father-in-law said he would be glad to come down and get us as he did at Christmas. He was going to go to Arkansas and Oklahoma anyway this fall on business, so he said the trip would suit him fine. These are all tentative plans, of course.

The weather has been very nice this past week. The daytime temperature has been averaging around 85 degrees. We have also received a substantial amount of rain; in fact, Sunday it rained close to three inches. The effect of rain in this part of Texas is much different than it is at home. It rains one day, and the next day it is dry and the ground becomes packed.

I sure hope everyone back home is fine. At this point it is not certain when we will be able to go on leave but it should be soon. Say hello to everyone for me. Give Bootsie's brood a big hug for me (Mom, you do this). Ha!

Bleib gesund und schreib bald wieder [Stay healthy and write again soon].

Roger

* * *

The previous letter was the last available piece of correspondence Buchta wrote home prior to his departure for Vietnam. Following completion of his basic combat training in late December 1966, Roger was allowed to return home for a brief period of leave and enjoy Christmas at home prior to reporting for his medical training. Likewise, he was able to return home for several days to be with family and his beloved animals prior to leaving the country for service in Vietnam. Confirmation of the next step in Roger's journey overseas came in the form of a postcard the soldier sent to his family with a postal date stamp of October 24, 1967, which was mailed from Oakland, California. In the brief space allowed for communication, Roger informed his parents and brother that he had arrived safely on the West Coast and met up with "three or four boys from my old company." He also remarked that he had gone through all the requirements to process for deployment and was on a standby status, awaiting final word on his specific departure date to be sent to a hospital in Long Binh, Vietnam. Once his flight arrived in Vietnam, and he received assignment to his permanent duty station, Roger assured his family that he would write home as soon as possible. Finally, he remarked that he believed his chances for an early discharge were good and went on to optimistically explain that he hoped he could return home in time to enroll at Lincoln University in the fall of 1968 to begin working toward his master's degree.

When preparing to depart the West Coast bound for service in Vietnam, this postcard was the last piece of correspondence the family of Buchta received from him while he was in the United States. The next piece of communication they received would arrive from Vietnam more than two weeks later.

On an interesting note, the aforementioned postcard arrived more than two weeks after Buchta had already reached Vietnam. His family received confirmation that their soldier arrived in-country on October 9, 1967, through a Military Affiliate Radio System (MARS) "radiogram." Now known as the Military Auxiliary Radio System, MARS was comprised of volunteer amateur radio operators worldwide who supported the various branches of the armed forces. Although the primary focus of MARS is "providing contingency communications support to the Army and Department of Defense," the MARS network allowed many soldiers serving in overseas locations, such as Vietnam, to communicate with family at home via phone patches in addition to having messages relayed from their service site to a MARS operator in their home community, who then provided the typed communication to the family.[39]

In his MARS radiogram, Buchta noted that, although he had arrived safely at Long Binh, his orders had since been altered, and he was instead being sent to work in a hospital in the nearby community of Qui Nhon. There was certainly a medley of both intriguing and disturbing occurrences on the international scene shortly before and after Roger's arrival. These events included a contentious presidential election on the horizon and a war effort that "had begun to bog down with neither side gaining anything but an ever-increasing casualty list."[40] Military intelligence realized that the conditions were ripening for the unleashing of a major offensive by the North Vietnamese, while soldiers at the lowest levels of the command chain, including Private Buchta, recognized a deadly event was about to unfold after the turn of the new year; an event that would soon be known as the Tet Offensive.

---

[39] Vergun, *Army's Military Auxiliary Radio System*, https://army.mil.
[40] Welsh, *The History of the Vietnam War*, 91.

CHAPTER 3

Qui Nhon, Vietnam

"It seems like only yesterday I was leaving home and now I'm 10,000 miles from home and have been here for three weeks already. Over here one seems to lose all conception of time. The war doesn't stop at night or during weekends so you can see how easily it is to lose track of time."
– Pvt. Buchta in a letter home shortly after his arrival in Vietnam.

S outh Vietnam had an agrarian attractiveness that appeared to resonate with a keen-eyed soldier who had spent his early years living and working on a farm in rural central Missouri. Following his arrival in Vietnam, and completion of the assortment of mundane tasks associated with in-processing, Buchta was advised of his duty assignment and transferred to a military base that had been established near Qui Nhơn—a coastal city in central Vietnam. Upon arrival, Roger was placed in an ambulance company. Shortly thereafter, Roger received a promotion to the rank of private first class. The first personal communication he sent to his family after reaching his temporary overseas home is dated November 1, 1967, and it discusses in rather rich detail Roger's current circumstances. Here he includes observations of the Vietnamese locals he encountered. Sections of the letters showcased Roger's ability to breathe fresh perspective into everyday happenings when writing about the lush environment which surrounded him.

A flourishing interest in amateur photography evolves in his communications: Roger embarks upon meticulous ponderings regarding the type of camera that he should purchase and the most affordable methods for getting slides and photographs printed while stationed overseas. There is also an excitement that emerges when he shares with his family an unexpected opportunity to reconnect with old friends supplemented by his musings of the lush landscapes he witnessed upon his initial arrival in Vietnam. The young soldier began to assume the reflection of a tourist who was visiting overseas for the first time—an enthralling opportunity for someone who, before his military service, had never strayed far from home. The hypnotic allure of his new environment was a moderately deceptive welcome. He would soon discover this. In the ensuing weeks, Roger would transition from a sightseer in an exotic foreign land to a medic, as he underwent several moves in duty stations, while witnessing the bloodshed wrought during times of war.

* * *

Pfc. Roger Buchta
51st Medical Company (Ambulance)
APO San Francisco 96238
November 1, 1967

Dear Mom, Dad and Don:
I thought I would get you a few lines while the opportunity was here. I'm finally at a permanent station. It sure feels good to be settled down and know what's what. I believe I mentioned in my last letter that I'm a part of an ambulance company in a little town about twelve miles north of Qui Nhon. It is about 100 miles southeast of the famous area called Pleiku and about 200 miles south of the DMZ [demilitarized zone]. This area, in a radius of about seventy or eighty miles, is fairly secure. There has never been a major engagement in this area and that sure is consoling to hear. The area of Qui Nhon... where I am, is mainly composed of medical complexes and Korean detachments. It is also on the coast.
Our duties consist mostly of transporting patients and supplies... We are also on ambulance commitments at the pier and at the airfield in case of a crash. So, between calls, if there are any, we sleep.

There are always two men on each commitment. It is such a secure area we don't even carry a firearm, but I can use my ten hours of basic hand-to-hand [combat training] if necessary. Ha! We do have guard [duty] about twice a week, which is not much. We sit in watch towers about four hours a night. The place is so heavily mined a piss ant couldn't get through. There is also a radar on the heights along with MP [Military Police] stations. Once in a while, a dog trips a flare; that's about the only action there is around here.

The barracks are surprisingly good. Shower facilities are also good although there is no hot water. I guess you can't ask for too much. The food is the best I've eaten since I've been in the Army. There is a much better selection of food. The one big disappointment is the PX. Some of the prices are no better than in the states. Cameras, radios and recorders are much cheaper, however. The thing that is really hard to grasp is our maid service. Each morning Vietnamese come in and pick up our laundry. In the evening, our laundry is neatly stacked at the foot of our bed. They really do a good job. It costs us about five dollars a month and it's well worth it. The Vietnamese also work in the mess hall and do all the dirty work such as making bunkers, cleaning latrines and heavy construction work. I got a haircut from a Vietnamese barber yesterday. They do a pretty fair job if you can be patient. They survey your head like an artist. Every hair has to be just right. They also give a massage. It costs about thirty cents. It makes you feel a bit eerie when they use their razor but they're very trustworthy and courteous.

Yesterday I was sitting on my bunk reading when who should step in but photographer Bailey. We were so surprised we were speechless. When we left Fort Hood, we sighed and said, "Well, that's the last we'll see of Bailey," and now he's right beside me again. He's really a very good guy... It sure helps to know someone with whom you have served for a long time. There are also two other fellows from my company at Hood that are here. My company commander from Hood is also supposed to be stationed here... One fellow here told me he saw Boice, who is also an ambulance driver in this area. I know the unit and understand we go there often so that makes three of us who are still in contact with one another. I'm going to find out where Carman, Hall and Hainzer are. Their orders probably sent them to this area also because almost all the medics now are sent up here where there is a shortage of medical personnel.

Hope everything back hone is fine. I sure hope Girl is doing well... Let me know if Sissy's blindness increases. I'm going to try and get some ointment which may help ease the irritation. I'll also send some ointment for Bootsie's itch. The name of it is Tetracaine. If that doesn't help her nothing will.

Sometime when you can, take some pictures and send them to me... I'm going to price some

Polaroids and buy one and send it home. I've taken almost a whole roll of slides so far. I'm going to have Bailey send them to the states to be developed. Over here they do such a poor job and takes so long it is easier to send the film to the states. So, it may take a while for you to receive them. The first slides will just be of our area. But as I move around more, I should be able to get some fascinating shots. The landscape of Vietnam is breathtaking. I'll also get some shots of the farming in this area. It is very good earth in the valley and lends itself well to such crops as rice, sorghum and peanuts. Pineapple trees are also found almost everywhere. The cattle are also fat and treated well. They are eaten, however. Most of the cattle are similar to the Brahma stock. There are also jerseys here probably introduced by the French. Most of the people in this area are Catholics. In fact, there is a large mission and leprosarium here.[41]

Better close for this time. Write soon and stay on the right side.

Love,
Roger

* * *

---

[41] Buchta describes the leper colony in nearby Quy Hoa, which was established in the 1920s and was operated by Franciscan sisters until 1975. The colony is still in operation, is located on the beach and even has restaurants and shops that are open to the public.

One of Buchta's initial observations in his previous letter relates to the South Vietnamese civilians cleared to perform various tasks on the base in Qui Nhon, which includes those providing laundry services and haircuts. Many veterans, returning from the war, have shared that, although the South Vietnamese were allies to the United States, the lines between them and the North Vietnamese and Viet Cong later became blurred as the outcome of the war became more uncertain, causing many to become distrustful of anyone who appeared Vietnamese. Although the military made every effort to evaluate the civilian personnel allowed to work on bases, stories began to circulate of enemy troops who were able to infiltrate the U.S. military support system and then attempted to kill U.S. troops. In an environment consisting largely of guerilla warfare tactics, such stories, whether founded, fiction or a mixture thereof, tended to spread quickly. Such seems to be the case in Buchta's mentioning of his initial discomfort when receiving a haircut by a South Vietnamese barber using a razor.

Private First Class Buchta also remarks on the "famous" city of Pleiku in his previous letter, when describing the community located in the Central Highlands of Vietnam. Buchta's description of Pleiku is likely related to the marginal reputation it acquired during the Vietnam War—first, as the site of attack by North Vietnamese in February 1965, which, sadly, resulted in the deaths of eight Americans while more than one hundred were wounded. Several days later, twenty-three Americans were killed and twenty-one wounded in an attack against a U.S. installation in Qui Nhon, where Buchta was stationed on the date he wrote his letter. Pleiku grew into a well-known base for both American and South Vietnamese forces during the war; however, the city was nearly burned to ruin by fleeing South Vietnamese soldiers in 1975. In later years, Pleiku was rebuilt through the funding and efforts of the Soviet Union, and, although the area is considered safe to visit, there are limited distinguishing features or characteristics to make it a celebrated tourist destination.

Roger also remarked that he was stationed approximately two hundred miles south of the DMZ, which served as the acronym for the "demilitarized zone." Established in 1954, during the Geneva Conference, the DMZ was a temporary demarcation line between North and South Vietnam agreed upon with the implicit understanding that the line would later be dissolved following the reunification of the two countries. The line was recognized as a separation of two Vietnams near the 17th Parallel. "From the South China Sea to the village of Bo Ho Su the line followed the Ben Hai River, and from Ben Ho Su the line proceeded due west to the border of Laos."[42] As a component of the thirty-nine-mile-long demarcation line, a buffer zone was established along the demilitarized zone consisting of a strip of land five miles wide. There was to be no movement of military supplies or equipment across the DMZ; however, this temporary line of separation between two countries became an enduring fixture when the United States continued to recognize the sovereignty the Republic of Vietnam—also known as South Vietnam. Throughout the Vietnam War, the neutral stance associated with the DMZ was regularly violated by all sides.

* * *

---

[42] Tucker, *The Encyclopedia of the Vietnam War*, 278.

Pfc. Roger Buchta
51st Medical Company (Ambulance)
APO San Francisco 96238
November 10, 1967

Dear Mom, Dad and Don:

I received your letter on Wednesday about four days after you sent it. You noted that you received mine in about three days. This is really much better service than I had expected. Instead of sending you a written letter, I was going to send you a taped letter. A few days ago, I purchased a little electric Panasonic tape recorder for $22.00 at the PX. I noticed that several fellows had purchased this particular brand (Japanese). This brand is sold throughout the world and parts are obtainable at any radio-TV repair shop. I was really impressed with the quality of this brand. When I get a chance, I will record letters and send them home. The tapes only cost 45 cents and there is no postage on them. Although the reels are small you can play them on your large tape recorder.

Perhaps I can shed some light on this area in which I'm stationed. So, I will devote a page or two on what I've observed and learned about this area in the short time that I have been here. Qui Nhon (Quin-yon) is a city on the coast with a civilian population of about 100,000... Qui Nhon is a major military base in Vietnam although you hear very little about it in the news. One of the major com-

mand headquarters is found in this city. There aren't many infantry units based in the area. Qui Nhon is mostly a supply area. Through its port come the supplies that are used by units in the northern part of Vietnam. There is also a large airport here. About twenty miles south of Qui Nhon they are building an airstrip that can and will be used for commercial airlines on which the military heavily depends for transporting troops from the states. Qui Nhon is probably best known for the 55th Medical Group, which has the major part of its support units in this area. They range from hospitals to ambulance companies. Many casualties from direct ground action are evacuated by helicopter and are taken to hospitals in this area. The helicopters land about twenty yards from an evacuation hospital. We run over from our ambulances when they land and take the patients (by litter) to the casualty and recovery room of the hospital. They are given emergency care and either remain in that hospital or they are sent to another hospital in the area. That is where we, as drivers, come in. The copters also bring in civilian casualties and Vietcong. We take them to Vietnamese hospitals in the area. We drive not only for the hospitals but also for dispensaries, the airport in case of a crash, and the dock. Much of our work is concerned with merely transporting medical supplies from one medical unit to another. That is about the extent of our duties as ambulance drivers.

The area between Qui Nhon and Phu Toung is used primarily for farming. There are also many construction projects underway in this area. The projects range from the building of roads to laying sewage and water pipes. American construction firms hire thousands of Vietnamese. So, in a way, the people are helping themselves in providing a better way of life. The presence of the United States is having a positive influence on the people in that they are becoming aware of the fact that there is a better way of life. The majority of the people aren't aware of why the U.S. is in their country or that there is even a war in their country. They just want to live, make enough money, and, I hope, learn something from the U.S.

Phu Toung is not really a city; it is really a military area composed of three or four compounds. There is a transportation battalion, a couple of huge construction units, a medical unit and warehouses... It is in a valley. The mountains... are behind my barracks. The mountains made me a bit uneasy at first but I understand there are numerous military units on the other side of the mountains and all through the mountains, for that fact. The Koreans patrol the mountains constantly. There are also radar emplacements and planes flying overhead 24 hours a day. Their area has never been attacked. Phu Toung is on a highway leading to Pleiku. It is heavily traveled night and day. The map below might help clarify the area somewhat.

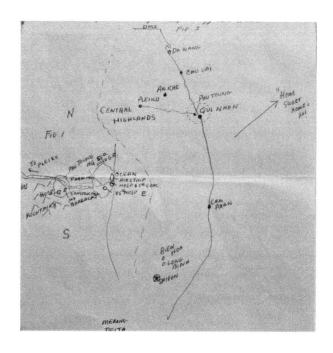

The hospital in Phu Toung is what is known as a clearing hospital. This means that it is mobile. In a matter of a few hours, the hospital can move where it is needed. It is completely made up of tents. There was some rumor that some of us would be transferred to this unit but nothing has materialized. All the men assigned to this hospital do is care for the equipment and be ready in case they are needed somewhere. It is a pretty good unit as far as work is concerned.

I hope I have given you some idea of the area in which I'm stationed. Perhaps when I become better acquainted with this region, and its significance, I can give you a more coherent picture.

If you get a chance, see if you can find me a booklet (self-teaching type) on the basic expressions of the Vietnamese language. I would very much like to learn some of the basic expressions. One of the major problems among the different foreign countries in Nam is that of communication. You may be able to find such a book in a bookstore. I have tried to find something over here but, surprisingly enough, there simply isn't anything. It seems the military would make some kind of effort to bridge the language gap between the two peoples because after all, that is where good relations have to begin... The Army offers correspondence courses in the language but it wouldn't be necessary to go deeply, so to speak, into the language. So, if you come across such a booklet some time, send it to me. Like Andy Griffith would say, "I'd 'preciate it."

I was glad to hear Quarry defeated Patterson even though there was some question... It was most heartwarming to hear that Girl is progressing well. I sure wish I could see her.

Better draw to a close for this time. Write when you can and say hello to every one for me.

Love,
Roger

* * *

In a number of his communications to family back in Missouri, Buchta refers to the Korean military members who served in Vietnam. Early in the United States' involvement in the Vietnam War, the South Vietnamese government made a request for military assistance to the Republic of Korea (South Korea). The request was fulfilled, and South Korea deployed their first troops to the region in 1964, several months before the arrival of the first wave of combat troops from the United States. As U.S. involvement continued to grow in Vietnam, President Lyndon Johnson issued a formal request for additional troop commitments from the South Koreans. Eventually, the South Korean forces would agree to subordinate their units to the American military command structure. Republic of Korea (ROK) forces would total approximately 300,000 during the war and included varying types of units such as medical teams, engineers, military police and a force specializing in counterinsurgency operations. It is estimated "about 5,000 South Korean soldiers died in the Vietnam War, and some returned with injuries and ailments caused by exposure to defoliants such as Agent Orange, which were employed by U.S. forces to kill the dense jungle that provided cover to the Viet Cong."[43]

While continuing to provide his intuitive personal observations regarding his Vietnam experiences, Buchta remained in his assignment to the 51st Medical Company, serving primarily in the capacity as an ambulance driver. The frenetic pace of operations was well underway in the months prior to Buchta's arrival in country since, in March 1967, the company was already credited with providing "ground medical support for 18 combat missions" and the evacua-

---

[43] Borowiec, *Allegations of S. Korean Atrocities*, May 16, 2015 edition of the *Los Angeles Times*.

tion of "more than 37,000 troops with most of the medical missions taking place on the bumpy and hazardous roads of Vietnam's Central Highlands."[44] The 51st Medical Company, according to Department of Army records, was later awarded the Meritorious Unit Citation for service while attached to the 71st Evacuation Hospital and was deactivated in Vietnam on October 1, 1970.

Buchta brought home from Vietnam this patch for the 51st Medical Company, to whom he was initially attached upon his arrival in Vietnam.

The great distance from home does not prevent the young private from expressing concern for his dogs and, on recurring occasions, inquiring of their condition. He also takes the time to make small talk about a boxing match that captured the attention of many sports fans in the U.S.—Floyd Patterson facing Jerry Quarry at the Olympic Auditorium in Los Angeles on October 28, 1967. The highly promoted event was a rematch from four months previous, when the two pugilists met at Memorial Coliseum for the first time and their fight ended in a draw. Quarry prevailed in their second match through a majority decision in the twelfth round.[45]

* * *

---

[44] March 31, 1967 edition of the *Tribune* (Scranton, Pennsylvania).

[45] BoxRec, *Floyd Patterson vs. Jerry Quarry*, www.boxrec.com.

Pfc. Roger Buchta
51st Medical Company (Ambulance)
APO San Francisco 96238
November 17, 1967

Dear Mom, Dad and Don:

Another week has passed—another week closer to the end. I guess I have about forty-four weeks remaining, which sounds like a frightfully long period of time. Back at Ft. Hood, those that had returned from 'Nam said the time passes quickly, and it seems that I have to agree. It seems like only yesterday I was leaving home, and now I'm 10,000 miles from home and have been here for three weeks already. Over here one seems to lose all conception of time. The war doesn't stop at night or during weekends, so you can see how easily it is to lose track of time. At Christmas and New Year there may be a truce, at least it is being proposed to the Vietcong by the government of South Vietnam. The United States is a bit leery of truces, because it gives the communists time to move supplies, and troops, and to rebuild. During the holidays there are generally no large missions or dispersal of troops. This, of course, gives the VC time to move troops and supplies. Unfortunately, they must not like Bob Hope and his troupe. I sure hope I get to see him at Christmas but you know how things are in the Army.

This week has been rather hectic. We moved to the 542nd even though there is no room. They jammed eleven of us into an area about as large as our dining room and kitchen. We don't have foot or wall lockers. It is not only uncomfortable but unhealthy when you cram this many people into so small an area. We are still on alert to move out. If we do, it will only be temporary, and we'll return here. In fact, we are leaving most of our possessions here and are taking only the necessities if we go. About all we are doing now is busy work. It is really worse than if we were doing nothing at all. So, I wish we would do something.

In about ten weeks I'm going to take my first seven days of R&R. At this point. I'm leaning heavily toward Australia; however, Bangkok seems to be the most popular place for R&R. Many fellows also go to Hong Kong and Tokyo. Sidney is not too popular because the standard of living is much higher than the other places, and it takes longer to get there. Then, too, the other places are more exotic if you like the Orient. But 'Nam is essentially Oriental as I want to get.

Enclosed is a money order (two) for $180. Detract what I owe you for the loan and for Girl and put the remainder in the bank. So long for this time. Hope you received my tape. I'll try to make another tape when I can.

Love,
Roger

* * *

Looking forward to brighter times in his military journey, Private First Class Buchta maintains some levity when discussing his upcoming R&R in a few weeks, and considerations regarding where he should invest his time away from his military responsibilities. His previous communication also reveals his recent reassignment to the 542nd Medical Company and the associated tight quarters in which he is required to live. These lighter remarks notwithstanding, the most poignant of his comments pertains to the truce. He notes that a truce is being discussed between the United States and the communists.

The Tết Holiday is the most revered of holidays for the Vietnamese people, a celebration of their new year. Based upon the lunar calendar, the holiday can extend between seven and nine days. Although Buchta was correct in that a truce was being publicly discussed for the holiday, which fell only a few weeks after the Christmas holiday, General William C. Westmoreland, who was at the time commander of American forces in Vietnam, expressed his own set of concerns regarding the truce. Westmoreland affirmed that "U.S. intelligence knew the North Vietnamese and Viet Cong were going to attack in a number of places during the holiday, but the offensive was greater than expected. He further explained, "Despite advance warnings, 50 percent of the South Vietnamese forces were on leave to be with their families for Tet."[46]

* * *

---

[46] January 31, 1988 edition of the *Journal News* (White Plains, New York).

Pfc. Roger Buchta
542nd Medical Company (CLR)
APO San Francisco 96238
November 26, 1967

Dear Mom, Dad and Don:

I received your newspaper yesterday. It was dated November 5th. Although it took about twenty days to receive, I found many articles that were very interesting especially the (St. Louis) Post-Dispatch picture magazine, which was dedicated to the fiftieth anniversary of the Bolshevik Revolution.[47] Life devoted one of its issues to the anniversary, but the picture magazine was much better. I also read the issue of Sports Illustrated which carried the article on the Quarry-Patterson fight. The article sure gave Patterson a buildup, and I supposed he deserved it.

Saturday all the trucks were loaded. So, the chances are pretty good the unit will go to the field. The location is classified. The unit is supposed to be in the field for a short period of time. When the infantry goes out on a mission, medical units such as I'm in provide medical support. There are usually two or three doctors attached to the hospital. The purpose of this type of hospital is to provide first-aid to casualties coming directly from the scene of the action. From the field hospital they are taken by

---

[47] Buchta refers to the *St. Louis Post-Dispatch*, a daily newspaper still in operation.

helicopter to an evacuation hospital. If the casualties are only slightly wounded, they stay at the hospital, which has ward facilities and then are sent back to their units. If the location for the hospital would take too long to go to by convoy, the trucks and men will go by plane and convoy from there to their hospital site.

The men in the unit just take the bare necessities. Everything else is locked up until the men return. The unit found out that it was scheduled to move by a rather short notice. You couldn't imagine the incompetence, stupidity, and chaos that prevailed on the part of the NCOs in charge of loading trucks and getting ready to move. There are almost more NCOs in the company than men to command. They contradict each other's orders and tempers begin to flare. It is really something to experience. The unit finished preparing to move about 2:00 Saturday afternoon. That evening the battalion had a barbecue. They had a trailer full of beer and three cases of liquor. From Saturday evening until the next morning, there was nothing but pure anarchy in the compound. Almost everyone was bombed out of his mind. The doctors and the NCOs were the worst ones. One doctor passed out and had to be put to bed. The other doctors, however, had a hard time getting him there due to their own conditions. It was a real wild party if you can call it that.

I received the pictures that you sent me last week. Overall, they came out pretty well. I was somewhat surprised to hear that you bought a Polaroid camera at Wrights.[48] *I checked into these cameras at the PX and was going to advise you not to buy one due to the high cost of the film and the camera's lack of versatility. You're paying about sixty cents each (color) print while I'm paying about thirty cents for mine. What I thought about doing was to buy a good camera at the PX and send mine home. The PX has a tremendous selection of cameras, both American and Japanese brands. Bailey, who is a professional photographer, said that the Japanese cameras are the best in the world. In fact, he said he would use nothing else. The Japanese cameras cost less than half what one would pay in the states. They are also versatile. You can take everything from portraits to pictures of birds and wildlife. The quality and cost of prints and slides also makes them very popular. I was going to advise you to buy a projector instead of a Polaroid, but I was a little late. Perhaps I can get a projector before I get out of the service. I sent a roll of slide film to a Kodak laboratory in Hawaii, so it should come back in the next few days. As soon as they come, I'll briefly explain the significance of each one and send them home.*

---

[48] The former Wright Studio & Camera Shop was located in Jefferson City, Missouri.

*I better hang it up for now… Give everyone
my regards and also give me an account of Girl's
progress. Also report on Sissy's problem.*

Love,
Roger

* * *

The former college student's love of world history is again displayed through his assessment of the articles regarding the fiftieth anniversary of the Bolshevik Revolution. This historic and, in many aspects, bloody moment in Russian history became a subject that he would refer to on numerous occasions when teaching world history in later years. His letter also provides a rather unvarnished appraisal, by a well-educated soldier, regarding the poor leadership in his company. He bemoans the incompetency that appeared to be the hallmark characteristic of their movement to the field in preparation for setting up the medical facilities that would soon be used in treating wounded infantry soldiers. Additionally, Buchta often confided to his brother during their conversations many years after the war that one aspect of living and working in a medical environment that became prevalent were the moments that devolved into debauchery, when parties erupted, and alcohol of all sorts flowed freely. In a non-judgmental manner, Buchta often remarked that such occurrences provided the personnel a form of escape from the horrors they were forced to endure as part of their daily routines.

At this point in his military journey, Buchta remained attached to the 542nd Medical Company. A lineage of the company notes it was initially constituted on April 3, 1944, and later earned a Meritorious Unit Commendation for its stellar performance during the Korean War. The company was disbanded in the fall of 1951 but was then reconstituted in 1953. During its service in the Vietnam War, the company was credited for its participation and medical support in several integral campaigns including the Tet Offensive.[49]

* * *

Pfc. Roger Buchta
542nd Medical Company (CLR)
APO San Francisco 96238
November 26, 1967

Dear Mom, Dad and Don:

Thanksgiving is over—Christmas is well under way. We had a delicious Thanksgiving Day dinner. It included the traditional turkey and dressing, cranberry sauce, desserts, and salads. The military goes all out in providing good holiday meals. It is going to be strange to celebrate Christmas away from home this year. The temperature will be in the 90s; the foliage will be green as ever and the growing season for truck crops and rice will be at its peak. But from the beer halls and radio one can already hear Bing Crosby singing "White Christmas" and "The

---

[49] United States Army Center of Military History, *542nd Medical Company*, https://history.army.mil.

Little Drummer Boy"—my favorites. One can even sense the spirit of the season from the Vietnamese girls who come and do the washing and cleaning all day. As I mentioned before, there are very many Vietnamese Catholics in this area. I understand they really go all out for Christmas. So, I guess Christmas is about the same everywhere there are Christians.

At the present time, part of our unit is moving out to a destination unknown. All we do know is that it is somewhere very near Saigon. It will take six transport planes to take us to Ben Hoa; and from there we'll convoy to the campsite. Each plane carries a 2-1/2-ton truck (loaded of course) plus the driver and four other men. It is remarkable how a plane can carry such a load. Two planes have already left, two more leave tonight, and we'll leave tomorrow. I'll be on the sixth, and last, plane. I understand we are supposed to support some infantry unit near Saigon and possibly be attached to another hospital in the area. I am eager to go into Saigon if I get a chance. In that case, I'll get some pretty good shots. Everyone got a good supply of film, including myself. It is really funny to see all these guys dressed in their battle gear with a big camera case hanging around their shoulders. I like my little Instamatic because it is so small, I can put it in my shirt pocket. As soon as I get to the campsite, which should be tomorrow, I'll take some slides of the hospital. It is composed of twelve tents, three doctors, and about forty men. I have been assigned as a clearing station attendant, which means I'll have the same duties as a medic giving shots, waiting on the patients, and preparing them for further evacuation, if necessary. It will probably be a tiring time for all of us. I don't have any idea how long we'll be in the field, but it shouldn't be longer than two or three months at the most. The time should pass quickly.

We have had some pretty good entertainment at the enlisted men's club the last few days. Sunday night a country and western band from Japan performed and some performance it was. The band consisted of three men and two girls—and what girls! One girl did most of the singing. She was an absolute goddess! They played all the favorite country songs, including a medley by Hank Williams. The boys from the South really ate it up. One of them hung a Confederate flag above the stage. When the band played "Dixie," they all stood at attention and saluted the flag. It was really something to see. The band was very talented and worthy of playing at the Grand Ol' Opry any day if they haven't already. They have performed in the United States many times.

Tuesday night a popular music group performed at the club. Michael Landon's (Little Joe) father was the leader of the group. Little Joe's sister was the lead singer. Last year she was the first runner-up in the Miss California beauty contest.

Besides these two, there were four boys and a Go-Go dancer from Israel. The show contains a comedy routine between Little Joe's father and daughter. It was typical GI humor, if you know what I mean. The music was pretty good, although it was too loud. The fellows really enjoyed it.

I'm sending a money order with this letter for $240. As a Pfc., I make about $182 a month. The other $60 was part of what I brought with me and what I didn't need last month. I sent some Christmas cards to several people. I picked out two that I was going to send to you and grandma a little later. In the confusion, they were lost. So, take out about $20 from these money orders. I was going to send some gifts home but I simply didn't have a good chance. Buy grandma a nice card and gift for me and buy each of you a little something. Perhaps you can also buy the dogs each a sack of food and get Girl a nice collar. I really hate that it has to be this way, but I hope you'll understand.

I better close for now. Hope everyone is fine. As soon as I get to my new station, I'll drop you a few lines and tell you what it is all about. Write when you can.

Roger

* * *

While he begins to settle into his new routines with the U.S. Army in Vietnam, Buchta's letters resonate with a more positive tone as he describes the celebration of this first holiday overseas, Thanksgiving, and then submits some observations regarding the activities and buzz unfolding with the approaching Christmas holiday. He also relates to his family the camaraderie that is developing between many troops experiencing the same set of military circumstances and who happen to be from other locations throughout the United States. This includes his Southern friends who enjoyed the musical interpretations of a Japanese band, that entertained the troops with their renditions of popular country and western music songs, both past and present. It is during this period, Buchta goes on to explain, that his duties as a medic now take on responsibilities that appear more focused on direct patient care rather than operating an ambulance or the patient transport tasks that defined his efforts in previous weeks.

Within only a week from the date of his previous letter home, Buchta and his company would move south and join their fellow hospital staff in preparing for the coming battles that quickly filled their wards with wounded and injured patients. Politically, this timeframe was quite interesting and uncertain since President Lyndon Johnson, who had ushered the nation into full-fledged conflict in Vietnam, learned that he would have an opponent in the Democratic primaries when Senator Eugene McCarthy announced his intention to run on November 30, 1967.

Though much activity was yet to come regarding the effects of the war on the local field hospitals, Buchta's letters to his family signaled rather lackluster activities, since casualty levels seemed to have diminished to a trickle of what they had been in previous weeks.

However, it was simply a matter of time before a resurgence of enemy activity in the area resulted in increased casualties being treated at the hospital. Statistics reveal that "(b)y the end of 1967, the U.S. troop presence was up to nearly a half million, an increase of a hundred thousand during the year, and American soldiers killed in action exceeding nine thousand—bringing total battlefield deaths for the past two years to more than fifteen thousand."[50] The country quickly became weary of the war when submitted to watching news footage of their boys being killed in action for a cause and purpose they did not fully comprehend. It may have begun as a relatively quiet period for Buchta and the hospital staff with whom he worked, but as the old saying goes, which the medic had likely heard many times from folks back in mid-Missouri, it was simply the "calm before the storm."

---

[50] Karnow, *Vietnam: A History*, 512

CHAPTER 4

Parties and Casualties

"We have taken over a large dispensary and a small hospital. The dispensary receives casualties directly from the field. There is a huge helicopter field across the road from the dispensary and hospital. Most of the casualties come in by 'copter." – Buchta describing Cu Chi, Vietnam in a letter home dated December 13, 1967.

T he war began to grow much closer for Buchta after he reached Cu Chi in the final days of November 1967. In a letter to his family, Roger noted that the expansive base covered an area that he estimated to be approximate to the size of the Jefferson City, Missouri and was also home to the 25th Infantry Division. The division had certainly endured a baptism of fire since leaving Schofield Barracks, Hawaii, in late 1965 and after establishing their base camp at Cu Chi in January 1966. When statistics were released in January 1967, nearly a year prior to Buchta's arrival at the base, the division had already suffered "617 killed and 4,198 wounded in some of the dirtiest battles of the war" following their arrival in Cu Chi. Major General Fred C. Weyand, who served as commanding general of the 25th Infantry Division, explained that the division became the largest combat force in Vietnam during this timeframe because of several brigades that had been attached in support of their combat mission. He further described Cu Chi as a "tough assignment" since it "had long been a sanctuary for the Viet Cong," which then required "several weeks of fierce fighting" to secure the base camp.[51]

The area surrounding the base, Buchta described, was rich land that appeared ideal for growing rice and was understandably deemed as valuable by the North Vietnamese. Additionally, in describing the camp, which had been won by the blood of many soldiers belonging to the 25th Infantry Division, he further explained that it remained a heavily fortified area with an active presence of Viet Cong troops in the surrounding areas. There were occasions, Buchta noted, when Viet Cong managed to sneak their way past the defensive perimeter

---

[51] January 8, 1967 edition of the *Honolulu Advertiser*.

but failed in their endeavor thanks to watch dogs (wolf hounds) that alerted guards to their presence. During the evening hours, in addition to maintaining an active perimeter, regular artillery attacks were launched against the Viet Cong in an attempt to prevent any assaults against the base. This constant barrage provided a consistent, thundering soundtrack for those who were stationed there. Helicopters were also a frequent sight and sound in the skies above the base, which Buchta described as "beautiful" and were credited with having saved the lives of many wounded soldiers.

The accommodations on Cu Chi may have initially appeared rather sparse for the medical soldiers, who were assigned to hooches that Buchta described as similar to "scratch-sheds for chickens" he had seen back home, but he realized that in light of their circumstances, that he had been given much better duty than most of his fellow soldiers, who were being sent into the jungle for dangerous combat missions. Shortly after his arrival at Cu Chi, Roger began working eight-hour shifts inside a small, air-conditioned hospital with approximately sixty patients, while the temperatures outdoors would often soar to a sweltering 110 degrees. There were movies shown every evening, and the post exchange was much larger and offered many more products and items than had been available in Roger's previous duty location. All things considered; the medic admitted his life in a combat zone was not all that unpalatable.

* * *

Pfc. Roger Buchta
542nd Medical Company, 3rd Platoon
Cu Chi, Vietnam
December 13, 1967

Dear Mom, Dad and Don:

It's a calm Wednesday night here in Cu Chi. Occasionally one can hear a few artillery rounds being fired, but other than that it's peaceful. The medical unit has been here in Cu Chi now for about two weeks. Almost everyone in the unit, including myself, really like it here, particularly from the standpoint of duty. We have taken over a large dispensary and a small hospital. The dispensary receives casualties directly from the field. There is a huge helicopter field across the road from the dispensary and hospital. Most of the casualties come in by 'copter.

Before going into more detail, perhaps I can explain what our unit is doing here. The unit that was in charge of the dispensary and hospital before we came has assumed other duties. As a result, the 542nd, or the third platoon to be more precise, has taken over the dispensary and hospital. Each of us were assigned duties connected with the two. I have been assigned to the wards. Only two wards are in use at the present time. Each ward is a round-type structure, which I suppose one could refer to as a Quonset hut. I have seen farm machine sheds that resemble them. Each ward can accommodate about *twenty patients, although there is seldom more than a half-dozen in each ward at a time. The reason there are so few at a given time is because only patients with mild illnesses and injuries are admitted here. Most of the casualties are here with shrapnel wounds or sprained ankles, problems of this nature. There are six of us assigned to the wards. Each of us works one eight-hour shift a day. It is very easy work. We give shots, change dressings, and things of this nature. The men who are seriously wounded go to a larger hospital in the area. The unit has two doctors. Both seem to be real nice guys. They are both orthopedists. At the dispensary, they perform minor surgery and give first aid to casualties prior to their disposition to a larger hospital. The NCOs and specialists work in the dispensary. Another good point about our present station is the fact that we don't pull any extra duties including guard, which can be a pretty hairy job. That's one advantage of being assigned to an infantry group.*

Cu Chi is the base camp of the 25th Infantry Division. It's about twenty miles from Saigon and is part of the famous Iron Triangle. There is much VC activity in this area. The land is very flat and marshy. The VC have been hard to defeat in this area, mainly because of their sophisticated bunker system. Lately, however, the US and South Vietnamese have been achieving some very significant victories in this area. It is only a matter of time before the VC lose complete control of the area.

There are many defections. The vast tunnel networks are steadily being found and destroyed. Cu Chi has been mortared twice this year, but there was very little damage. All night one can hear artillery firing, mainly for purposes of harassment. Flares go off periodically around the camp. Overall, though, I guess it is about as safe as any area in Vietnam.

The camp has certain advantages over Qui Nhon. There is a huge post exchange where one can purchase many things that weren't available in Qui Nhon. For recreation there is a large pontoon-type swimming pool. They also have miniature golf, basketball, and a few other outdoor sports. It is also very uncrowded in this camp. When you walk around the place it looks like a ghost town. The different units come in from the field about one or two days a week, so there is a certain amount of privacy.

We are supposed to be here at least through December; from there, no one knows. We may return to Qui Nhon or stay here for a while longer. Another possibility is that we may be going to the field. So, we have to just wait and see.

Well, it looks like Christmas is just a few days away. Packages are really beginning to come in. One fellow in my barracks received a small tree. We got some ornaments and decorated it. When each of us receives something from back home, we put it under the tree for Christmas. The hospital is also receiving some packages, mainly consisting of candies and cookies, from various church groups in the states. The mail got mixed up when we moved; as a result, I still haven't' received the box that you sent me yet. But we are beginning to receive mail that, of course, was sent to our old address.

In his communications home, Buchta referred to the hospital buildings at Cu Chi as "round-type" structures similar to those he had seen used as machine sheds back in Missouri. This is a photograph of such buildings retrieved from one of the slides the soldier sent home while in Vietnam.

I will close for now. This week I'm working on the night shift. About all I have to do is read and write. Thus, I'll write again soon. Write when you can.

Roger

* * *

Their base camp in Cu Chi, Buchta illustrated in his letters, was located near Saigon, which is now known as Ho Chi Minh City, in a region that was given the designation "Iron Triangle."[52] The 120-square-mile area comprising the Iron Triangle has been described as "a largely flat landscape covered by dense underbrush and tall elephant grass and known as War Zone 3."[53] Months before Buchta arrived in the area, a search-and-destroy drive, known as Operation Cedar Falls, had been launched that consisted of "sixteen thousand Americans and an equal number of South Vietnamese troops… designed to wipe out (the) communist stronghold… (in) the Iron Triangle."[54] Civilians were evacuated from the region prior to the operation. This was followed by unyielding shelling and bombing by U.S. forces, resulting in the elimination of four primary villages believed to have been used for concealment by enemy soldiers. However, enemy forces were alerted to the pending attack. Those unable to find protection in tunnels, fled the area. Months later, the Viet Cong troops returned to the area to reestablish a stronghold they would use when launching the Tet Offensive in the waning days of January 1968.

The bunkers in the vicinity of Cu Chi, referred to in Buchta's letters, have become something of legend. This vast network of tunnels, spanning an impressive 125 miles in total length, were accessed by enemy troops through a number of hidden entrances in the forests surrounding Cu Chi. These tunnels allowed one to move through the area virtually undetected. This strategic network of tunnels provided Viet Cong the ability to launch surprise attacks during the

---

52 See Appendix B.
53 October 11, 2019 edition of *The Post and Courier*.
54 Karnow, *Vietnam: A History*, 463.

Tet Offensive and other assault initiatives. The tunnels miraculously endured the intense bombing campaigns levied by U.S. forces during the Vietnam War. In recent decades, the tunnels have been preserved and developed into a top tourist attraction for the country, and they receive millions of visitors every year.

* * *

Pfc. Roger Buchta
542nd Medical Company, 3rd Platoon
Cu Chi, Vietnam
December 16, 1967

Dear Mom, Dad and Don:
I thought I'd drop you a few lines to let you know that I've received the reading material which you sent me. The material came at a very opportune time for me. This week I'm working on the night shift from 11 p.m. to 7 a.m. So, about all I have to do is read and write. This evening we got in some mass casualties. A South Vietnamese ranger squad was ambushed by VC and sent to our dispensary. There were ten of them. They had mostly shrapnel and bullet wounds. Most of them were in real bad shape. One that I was working with had a bullet hole through his stomach plus shrapnel wounds in both legs. We cut his clothes off, cleaned and dressed his wounds, and administered IV fluids. A couple had to have surgery on the spot. Our CO [commanding officer] and XO

[executive officer], both doctors of course, performed the operations. From the dispensary they were sent to a larger hospital. It was a bloody sight. I wish our beloved president could have been here. Shortly before I went on duty, they brought in a sergeant who was part of a demolition team that got hit by a claymore mine. Both of his thighs were badly mutilated. When a claymore mine explodes, it throws hundreds of steel spikes. You can't imagine what something looks like after it has been hit by such a mine. Many of the fragments had to be left in his legs. He's in my ward. The pains were so severe I had to give him Demerol, a narcotic pain killer, every four hours. Being unable to sleep, he related to me what had happened. It was some story. Most of the men are reluctant to discuss the incidences leading to their admission to the hospital. This is understandable.

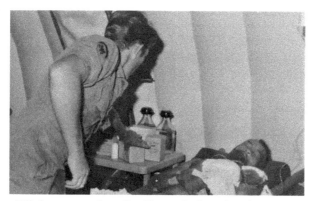

While stationed at Cu Chi with the 542nd Medical Company, Buchta and many of his fellow medics treated a variety of patients, including South Vietnamese military members who were wounded in combat.

When I came to work tonight, I was surprised to see the ward gaily decorated with Christmas ornaments—trees, wreaths, and Santa Clauses were everywhere. It seems the Red Cross ladies had really put in a hard day. Two women, both young and quite nice, visit the wards about every other day. They visit with the patients and bring them cookies and candy. The men really look forward to their coming.

Well, Christmas is just around the corner. On the radio they are beginning to play songs of the season. We are very close to Saigon, so reception is quite good. We can pick up the American stations. Both are military stations. One of them can probably compete with the radio stations in the states. Of course, there are no commercials. News and sports coverage are excellent. There are also interviews with famous people such as movie stars, singers, etc. Music ranges all the way from country and western to classical. Some programs, such as the Jack Wagner program, come from Hollywood. Then, too, every night at 9:00 there is the Chris Noel Program. She comes on with a smooth, seductive voice. One fellow said he gets turned on just listening to her. She plays mostly rock 'n' roll music.[55]

---

[55] Although Jack Wagner, who passed away in 1995, was best known as an announcer at Disneyland and his voice work with Walt Disney World Resort, he also worked in radio with KNX in Los Angeles in addition to acting in such television shows as *The Adventures of Ozzie and Harriet*. Chris Noel is an American model and actress who toured with Bob Hope twice during the Vietnam War. During the war, as referenced by Buchta, she also hosted her own program from the Armed Forces Network.

TV is something altogether different. The shows are mostly reruns, many of which I saw last summer. Football games are generally a week late. Most of the programs are of a poor quality except one, The Lawrence Welk Show. The Tonight Show and The Joey Bishop Show are also on, although they are several days late… It is really unbelievable to see The Tonight Show without any commercials. Overall, the TV is pretty poor.[56]

…I was happy to hear that Girl is doing well. In a future letter, perhaps you'll tell me how Sissy is coming along. I sure hope she doesn't go blind. You mentioned that Rudy got a couple of pretty large coons. I hope you can have an opportunity to take Blue out a little this winter. He'd better be ready next winter for damn sure. Of course, you can't expect too much from Blue, but he may come through if he gets a little experience.

I better close for now. If you don't receive any more letters from me before Christmas, I hope you all have a joyous holiday season. Say hi to everyone for me and write soon.

Roger

* * *

---

[56] *The Lawrence Welk Show* was a musical variety show that aired from 1955 to 1982. *The Joey Bishop Show* was an American sitcom that originally aired from 1961 to 1965. *The Tonight Show* is a talk show that first aired on NBC in 1954 with Johnny Carson fulfilling the role of host from 1962 to 1992.

The written conversations from Buchta regarding his experiences in Vietnam continued to oscillate between periods of intense hardship counterbalanced by more joyful reflections and moments. For instance, the young medic candidly describes, for his parents and brother, some of the egregious wounds that he had to treat and the intimate discussions he had with soldiers who were often hesitant to relate the circumstances that resulted in their specific injuries. He also chooses to illustrate in rather lurid detail how his duties on the ward have become more intense. He shares that he has assumed such additional duties as administering a greater number of IVs and narcotic painkillers. It is disheartening for the medic to have to see such young men close to his age—and some younger—wounded and in great distress, and he expresses a rare moment of anger at the president, wishing the commander-in-chief could be there at the hospital to witness first-hand the results of his decisions that are being made in Washington, D.C. At the time, one might not believe that exposure to such sights would have a long-term effect on Buchta. In later years, he, like many of the wounded soldiers he treated, grew reluctant to share any stories regarding his experiences in a combat zone.

On the flip side of the coin, Roger often expresses his longing for home, in a sense, by focusing some of his attention on the various programs of entertainment available on both the radio and television through broadcasts from Saigon. Such programs as *The Tonight Show*, hosted by iconic personality Johnny Carson, provide Buchta with a connection to family thousands of miles away, bringing more pleasant reflections to an otherwise traumatic environment. There is also the approaching Christmas holiday, now less than two weeks away, offering a glimmer of hope for the coming of brighter circumstances. As with many of his letters, Buchta inquires as to the current health conditions of the family's dogs and looks forward to participating in some raccoon hunting once he finishes his overseas tour and returns home to Missouri.

* * *

Sp/4. Roger Buchta
542nd Medical Company, 3rd Platoon
Cu Chi, Vietnam
December 19, 1967

Dear Mom, Dad and Don:

    I thought I'd drop you a few lines to let you know that I've received your package of cookies, cigarettes, tobacco, and tape. A fellow in my living quarters got a little tree from home. We decorated it with ornaments that we bought at the PX. Each time one of us receives a gift, we put it under the tree for Christmas. We are really accumulating a pile of gifts. The platoon is supposed to have a big Christmas party, so we are saving the cookies, nuts, candy, and other goodies. Some of the gifts received are really out of place. One fellow got two sweaters. To take the cake, though, one fellow got a coloring book. They rode that poor kid to death.

While serving in Vietnam, Buchta's parents mailed him several Ernest Hemingway novels, one of which he is pictured reading during his time-off from his medical duties with the U.S. Army.

Besides the wonderful gifts, which were sent to me from home, I got a pretty good gift from the Army. I got a promotion to Specialist 4 or E-4. In Vietnam, it is very easy to make rank. Actually, I stand a pretty good chance of making Specialist 5. The biggest jump, however, is from E-3 to E-4. It will mean about a $40 hike in pay... I should be able to save a fairly respectable sum of money by the time I get out of the Army. This month, so far, I've only spent about twelve dollars, and part of that was for a pair of prescription sunglasses. I ordered a pair of sunglasses from a Korean optometrist at the PX. All of the small businesses, or concessionaires, that *are attached to the PX are approved by the Army or they wouldn't be allowed to operate on post. Most of the businesses are Korean. They range from tailor shops to laundries to barber shops. The glasses cost me $13.90, which is considerably less than the $25 we have to pay for prescription glasses at home.*

Although I hope to save quite a bit of money, I'll have to hold some back for R&R. Then, too, I want to purchase such items as a ring, field glasses, and a slide projector before returning home.

I'm having some dental work done at the present time. One tooth was pulled and four filled. The gum cavity of the tooth that was pulled really hurt after the anesthetic wore off. I took a couple of pain capsules, which really did the trick…

I have been reading the paperback you sent me by Ernest Hemingway.[57] He is certainly a very interesting writer. One can see why he won the Nobel Prize for literature. It has been a long time since I read anything by him. If you want to read a good book, or series of articles, read "Twenty Letters to a Friend" by Svetlana Alliluyeva, Stalin's daughter, who recently fled to the United States. She tells about her infamous father during her childhood and at his death. I have never read anyone who could create

---

[57] Ernest Hemingway was awarded the Nobel Prize in Literature in 1954 "for his mastery of the art of narrative, most recently demonstrated in *The Old Man and the Sea,* and for the influence that he has exerted on contemporary style." The Nobel Prize, *Ernest Miller Hemingway,* https://nobelprize.org.

such feeling and write with such interest in a fiction or non-fiction work, as this woman has done. Life or Look [magazines] ran a series of selections from her book. This is where I came into contact with her works. Want to also give you a tip on a darn good movie, "The 25th Hour" starring Anthony Quinn and Virna Lisi. It is a story about a Romanian peasant and his family during the Second World War. It is well worth seeing. They have an outdoor theater about 100 feet from our living quarters where they show movies six nights a week. Most of the movies are current releases.

Better close for now and get a little shuteye. I received your newspaper dated December 3. Hope you all are fine and write when you can.

Roger

* * *

This final letter Buchta sends home to his family prior to Christmas is much more mirthful than the previous, with the soldier describing the preparations he and his fellow medics are making for the holiday. A large part of his joy likely comes from his recent promotion to Specialist 4, that resulted in a rather substantial increase in pay and will afford him the funds to make several purchases of items that interested him at the Post Exchange. By all appearances, Roger does seem to be enjoying some amenities of back home. Roger reports having frequent opportunities to watch recent movie releases, while also maintaining his penchant for reading books and articles that satisfy his entrenched interest in world history. In addition to his standard letter, Roger includes a Christmas card addressed to his family, that is steeped in detailed, colorful Vietnamese features. Inside the card, he notes that the Vietnamese operate a small gift shop near the Post Exchange on Cu Chi and sell items ranging from "ancient Oriental coins to straw hats." He further explains that a large part of the merchandise available at the shop is made in either Hong Kong or Japan, adding that if the South Vietnamese "could make war like they make money, we would be home for Christmas."

A Christmas Miracle

During a 2016 interview, Buchta discussed a number of fascinating details regarding a miraculous holiday occurrence that defined an extensive part of his memories from the war. It was one of only a handful of moments from his Vietnam experiences that Roger would choose to share with others in later years; however, he chose not to mention in his frequent letters home from the war.

"It was sometime around Christmas 1967, and there was a monsoon occurring that delivered strong winds that lashed against our rickety tents," recalled Buchta. "It was a slow time for those working in the hospital while the medics and nurses endured the monsoon by tending to the few patients recovering from surgery. When not occupied with other duties, many of us passed the time by playing cards, drinking coffee, and generally enjoying a break from the stress of receiving and preparing causalities for emergency operations."

The howling of the wind, and seemingly incessant splattering of the rain against the sides of the tents, was soon interrupted when an older Vietnamese man slowly opened the door to the emergency room, accompanied by a young Vietnamese woman, who appeared to be in a great deal of pain.

"We [medical staff] attempted to use our limited Vietnamese vocabulary to figure out the source of her discomfort," said Buchta, "but it was to no avail. Finally," he continued, "the man pointed to the lady's stomach and pretended as if he were rocking a baby— and that's when we realized she was ready to give birth. [A medical situation, he said, for which the medics were not trained to address.]

A nurse on duty quickly located one of the Army doctors, who fortunately happened to be an obstetrician. After examining the patient, the doctor announced that the woman would not only be giving birth once, but twice.

"The doctor proclaimed, 'She is going to have twins!'" recalled Buchta.

The doctor's assessment also revealed that the infants would be premature, which then resulted in the search for an incubator to ensure their survival. The medical unit staff were able to locate an incubator aboard a hospital ship anchored off the coast a short distance away, but, due to the storms ravaging the area, the helicopters needed to deliver the medical equipment were grounded. The approach of dawn brought with it a small glimmer of hope when the sun began to pierce the clouds. As the harsh weather began to subside, a pilot was located. He agreed to retrieve the incubator from the hospital ship.

"After a brief time, a nurse from the operating room opened the emergency room door and announced the lady was the mother of twin girls," Buchta smiled. "It was truly a novel experience for us all; after seeing and dealing with death and wounds day after day, this was new life… and, after all, it was Christmastime as well."

The new mother and her twin daughters were taken to the post-operation area; the twins were healthy enough that the incubator was never required. Through the assistance of an interpreter, the mother asked to see all of the emergency room personnel who cared for her throughout the delivery. She informed the staff she would like for them to name her children. Perplexed, the medics wondered what would be appropriate names for the girls when Buchta noticed the mother wearing a necklace with a cross.

"She was Catholic," Buchta explained, "and I suddenly thought, 'What about good strong Catholic names: Mary and Martha?'"

When the mother learned of the new names for her children, she was elated, Buchta noted—a joyous experience that served as the capstone event of the young medic's Christmas celebration of 1967 and the year he spent in Vietnam.

Decades may have passed since the birth of Mary and Martha during the Vietnam War, yet Buchta recalled that throughout the intervening years, he often wondered what became of the two young girls for whom he helped provide names.

"The girls were so small I remember holding each one in my hand," he said. "[The family] disappeared soon after the girls were born; the South Vietnamese military came and took them away. They were probably taken to the civilian hospital a few miles away," he added.

In late January 1968, North Vietnamese forces briefly overran much of the area and several other cities in what is known as the Tet Offensive—a coordinated effort to collapse the government of the Republic of South Vietnam. Though the enemy forces were quickly repelled, it was a memorable event for Buchta, who remains uncertain as to how the twins were affected.

"Sadly, I have no idea what became of the girls or their family, but being able to experience their birth is one of the better memories I have from my service and was a rather unique situation considering the combat environment to which we were accustomed."

* * *

Sp/4. Roger Buchta
542nd Medical Company, 3rd Platoon
Cu Chi, Vietnam
December 28, 1967

Dear Mom, Dad and Don:
Christmas is over and the new year is just around the corner. It really didn't seem like a Christmas that I'm accustomed to. Christmas Day

in Vietnam is really much like any other day. It seems nobody acknowledges the holiday, even though a "truce" is in effect. These truces are mistakes. While the U.S. stops offensive actions, the enemy moves supplies and men. As soon as the truce was over, all hell broke loose over Vietnam. Casualties are really heavy, so these truces are really ridiculous.

Our platoon did have a Christmas party. It was a typical Army party: soda, beer, liquor, and potato chips. We have three officers in our platoon: two doctors and a second lieutenant. They are all draftees and about as military-minded as I am. It wasn't much of a party. Everybody got bombed out of their minds, including the officers. One of them was demonstrating his jump shot from when he played college ball. In the process, he fell flat on his face. The other doctor was trying to check and see if he was hurt, but he was just one step away from collapsing himself. It was some party. I think I was the only one who stayed sober.

They really had a great Christmas dinner. There was more food than you could shake a stick at. The meal included the usual turkey and trimmings, vegetables, fruit cake, nuts, eggnog, and other holiday favorites. Each of us received a present from various organizations. Mine was from a Presbyterian church in North Carolina. The package included a couple novels, a comb, gum, a pen, and stationery. Of course, almost everyone has received a lot of cook-

ies and candy; so, we certainly had enough to eat. I received packages from you...

So, 1968 is on its way. I'm planning on getting an early separation in August, if all goes well. Pretty soon, I'll be short (200 days) and have to get me a short-timer's calendar. The time really seems to fly.

You sure must be having some real winter weather back home. According to the news on TV and radio, very few parts of the country have been spared from the cold and snow. It is almost unbelievable that they could have so much snow in Arizona. I have been keeping up with the plight of the Navajos. I can't imagine so much snow in a desert state. It is not too much like winter here. The old thermometer hits 95-plus mark every day.[58]

In your letter, dated the 21st, you noted that you have begun remodeling the dining room. I'm interested in knowing how you are going to remodel it. Perhaps you could drop me a few lines on that subject. I was glad to hear that Girl is doing well. Wonder if she knows what we did for her and she appreciates it. I think she does. In a future letter,

---

[58] The second week of December 1967 brought with it an unprecedented level of snowfall that impacted the Navajo Nation. A total of thirty-six inches of snow fell during the weather anomaly and resulted in rescue efforts by tribal, state and federal authorities. An estimated 60,000 Navajo were believed to be suffering from weather exposure and lack of food and the Air Force was called upon to assist in delivering provisions and supplies to those trapped in their homes. The emergency was declared over on December 27, 1967. The December 12, 2011 edition of the *Navajo Times*.

tell me how Sissy is coming along. If her eyes really bother her, let me know, and I'll send some ophthalmic ointment. It may ease the irritation. I'll also send some antibiotic ointment, which I'm certain will help Bootsie's rash.

Well, that's about all I have for now. Want to mention that I've received the packages and newspaper (December 17) that you sent me. Tomorrow Bob Hope is supposed to be here... I'm working on the night shift again this week, so I have plenty of time to read and write. Say hello to everyone for me and hope you all have a very happy New Year. Write soon.

Roger

* * *

With the Christmas holiday now several days in the past, the soldier does not mention to his family that within a few days he will be transferring to a new location, several hundred miles to the north. Likely, he had not been informed of the pending move, since many of the details were still in flux. However, the final days at Cu Chi were spent celebrating a quiet Christmas holiday, followed by a renewed outbreak of hostilities, resulting in casualties coming into their hospital. He commented on the failures and dangers of the truce, which, in his estimation, simply provided enemy forces the opportunity to rebuild and prepare for further combat. The truce was simply a cease-fire that lasted "for a few hours, or even a day or two, depending on where you were," wrote Vietnam veteran Joe Barrera in a column for *The Gazette* on December 23, 2018. He added, "The ceasefire had been announced by both the U.S. and South Vietnam. The Viet Cong and the North Vietnamese agreed to it, somewhat reluctantly. They immediately violated it, firing their ubiquitous mortars at U.S. base camps."[59] This version of circumstances parallels those described by Buchta, explaining the hopeless outcomes when the country's leadership chose to engage in such truces.

The brief delay in hostilities on Christmas did provide the hospital and medical staff many opportunities indulge in the spirits, consuming large amounts of alcohol, as Buchta noted in his writings. Roger served within a medical company comprised largely of draftees. He remarks that he did not fit the traditional mold of a soldier and alludes to the fact that many of his fellow medics, most notably the doctors, were simply in Vietnam (and the military) because they were compelled into service. The Christmas spirit for the soldier may have been slightly mitigated because of the hot weather and absence of the snow Roger experienced while at the military base, but he did mention briefly the opportunity to see the legendary Bob Hope when he visited Cu Chi on December 29, 1967. From 1964 to 1972, the comedian made trips to Vietnam to entertain the troops in various locations, giving performances that helped raise the spirits of the troops and provided them with a little taste of home. During his 1967 tour, Hope was joined by the beautiful American actress and singer, Raquel Welch, the latter of whom left something of an impression on Buchta.

---

[59] December 23, 2018 edition of the *Gazette*.

"Roger remembered the show quite well and was somehow lucky enough to get a seat in the second row," said Buchta's older brother, Don. "Not only did Roger have the opportunity to briefly visit with Bob Hope, but he also said that Raquel Welch was one of the most stunningly beautiful women he'd ever seen."

The comedian's shows always tended to be quite the impressive production with "a cloak of secrecy surround(ing) the tour... for security reasons," reported the *Stars and Stripes* when writing about one of his 1964 events. The magazine further noted, "Newsmen, given only a two-hour advance of the arrival, weren't even told where they were going until they were airborne out of Saigon. Military police were everywhere, and Hope, commenting on the security backstage, seemed amazed and appreciative. Even under a blistering sun that sent the temperature to 92 degrees, it seemed like Christmas when the cast ended the show with *Silent Night*."[60]

This welcome break from the monotony of war would soon fade to the background as the hospitals began to receive a massive influx of wounded troops during the emerging Tet Offensive. The rather lackadaisical military environment that Roger had enjoyed up to this point would disappear for several weeks, while Buchta and his fellow soldiers faced the horrors of treating scores of young men–and on occasion, Vietnamese children—horribly scarred and injured because of combat. Post-traumatic stress developed into a pervasive concern among American troops after the war, when many of the former service members who experienced the horrors of death and destruction on the frontline struggled to come to grips with its destructive effects. In later years, the young medic from Lohman,

---

[60] December 26, 1964 edition of *Stars and Stripes* magazine.

who previously had never experienced anything bloodier than delivering a calf on a farm during childhood, was now treating young men viciously mutilated while others less fortunate had to be prepared for body bags for their return trip to the United States, absent any parades for heroes received by previous generations of veterans.

CHAPTER 5

Unleashing the Storm

"When we arrived, we pitched three large tents in which to live. The unit is supposed to be in training here with the 18th Surgical Hospital for about two or three weeks. From there, the rumor is that we'll pick up two surgeons and assume the duties of a surgical hospital." – Buchta describing his arrival in Lai Khe in a letter home dated January 5, 1968.

A week following his last communication to family in Missouri became a demanding period for Buchta when the 542nd Medical Company packed up their belongings and entered the early days of 1968 by moving several hundred miles up the coast of Vietnam to the military base at Lai Khe. In a letter mailed home on January 5, 1968, Buchta explained that his company was already making preparations to receive a number of replacements since many of their lower enlisted soldiers were rotating back to the states after completing their overseas commitment. Additionally, he goes on to describe the tenseness that permeated the company and other personnel around the base since the medical units were "tightening up" in expectation that North Vietnamese forces were believed to be organizing one final and major offensive drive. Buchta's perception of developing events was based upon listening to conversations between others within the company, chatter around the base, and what little news about the war was being publicly disseminated at the time. He believed that the North Vietnamese were growing desperate in their efforts, and the war might end in a truce later in the year.

The base at Lai Khe was described by the soldier as a huge rubber plantation with both the buildings and natives lending evidence to the area's rich French influence and history. In his written ruminations, Buchta noted that many of the local population were fluent in the French language—a result of the European country's occupation of Vietnam many years earlier. Lai Khe, he went on to explain, served as the headquarters of the First Infantry Division, commonly referred to as the "Big Red One" because of the large numeral "1" on the shoulder patch worn by the soldiers of the division.[61] The camp, he added, was very primitive in appearance when compared to previous camps he had visited, composed primarily of row upon row of tents.

This photograph was copied from one of the many slides Buchta mailed home while in Vietnam, which shows part of the area assigned to the 542nd Medical Company following their arrival at Lai Khe in January 1968.

Located on the outskirts of Saigon, the Lai Khe Base Camp was considered part of the city's defensive perimeter. Additionally, because of its proximity to the deadly Iron Triangle, it became "a constant target for enemy attacks, and there were occasions when the camp received incoming rockets three times per day and twice per night. There was a sign at the main gate reading: 'Welcome to Rocket City,'" notes the Vietnam War Travel website.[62]

---

[61] The First Infantry Division was headquartered at Lai Khe from October 1967 to January 1970.
[62] Vietnam War Travel, *La Khe Base Camp*, https://namwartravel.com.

"When we arrived, we pitched three large tents in which to live," he wrote, in a letter home dated January 5, 1968. The unit is supposed to be in training here with the 18th Surgical Hospital for about two or three weeks. From there, the rumor is that we'll pick up two surgeons and assume the duties of a surgical hospital. Then, we'll set up a hospital of our own, probably in support of an infantry unit, but, of course, this is only speculation."

One challenging circumstance that enlisted soldiers have often suffered for time immemorial is the lack of information regarding their upcoming missions, activities, etc. In this spirit, Buchta bemoans the dearth of guidance he and his fellow soldiers of the company have received. Despite any deficit in news being shared, the uptick in preparatory activities of the hospital did not diminish the consumption of alcohol since, Buchta explained, the pay officer for the 542nd Medical Company recently arrived safely at Lai Khe, and the staff chose to celebrate his safe arrival through a little consumption of spirits. He mirthfully remarked, "One thing for sure, it doesn't take much to motivate our unit to have a party. During December we had about a half dozen." In addition to the levity their frequent parties provided, the soldier shared that, according to his calculations, he had about 221 days left in Vietnam and revealed that he was hopeful he might be able to secure an early discharge from the U.S. Army sometime around August 15, 1968.

* * *

Sp/4. Roger Buchta
542nd Medical Company
Lai Khe, South Vietnam
January 13, 1968

Dear Mom, Dad and Don:

I hope this letter finds everyone in tiptop shape on the home front. Everything seems to be progressing as usual in this part of the world. It is a calm Saturday evening here at Lai Khe. About all one hears is the constant hum of the big generators. Occasionally, a few helicopters drift overhead, but, other than that, all is quiet here on the Eastern Front. Actually, it has been pretty quiet in this area for the past few days. The first part of the week, there was quite a bit of activity in the area. One night about 3:00 a.m. the VC lobbed a few mortars on one side of the camp. Then they tried a ground attack. It was a futile effort. There was no one hurt during the mortar barrage and very few during the ground attack. It really seems ridiculous sometimes how the VC and NVA fight this damn war. They try to overrun a base camp with a very insufficient number of men. As a result, they have met with one defeat after another in the past few months. It seems almost as if they are making desperate moves, hoping for a miracle. So much for more grim aspects of the situation.

This week our unit began working with the 18th Surgical Hospital. This hospital is very large. There must be at least 100 personnel or more in the unit. This type of hospital performs all types of major surgery. From here, the patients get evacuated to larger hospitals either in Vietnam or back in the states.

While attached to the 18th Surgical Hospital in Lai Khe, Buchta often served inside of these inflatable, air-conditioned hospital units. He noted in his letters home that the insides of the hospitals were crowded and poorly organized.

This type of hospital is very unusual in that it is made of rubber, and it is inflatable. Huge generators provide power and air-conditioning for all the units. This type of set-up comes complete from the manufacturer. Everything is light and easily transportable. Tables, bedside stands, and desks fold up and fit on the sides of chests. One of the major problems in setting up such a hospital is finding where *everything is attached. It is like getting a hospital in a kit. All of the structures, generators, and equipment cost approximately $7,500,000. There are four such hospital in Vietnam. They are, more or less, in a trial stage. So, the cost of these structures gives you some idea where your tax money is going. In my next batch of slides, you'll see what these structures look like.*

I have been working on the wards; it is very unpleasant to work here. The structures are very overcrowded and poorly organized. The personnel of the 18th have been very rude, mainly because they are overworked. They seldom have time to show us anything. Our two doctors were really utilized when they arrived. Our platoon leader, or chief doctor, dropped into the tent a few minutes ago for a couple of beers. He said he hasn't had time for a shower in four days. He indicated that we would be leaving very soon, probably for Qui Nhon... In a way, I like to move around. One gets to see assorted pictures of Vietnam, and perhaps one can understand the situation a little better. On the other hand, you want to settle down and find some sort of a routine. I would like to go to Pleiku sometime. Pleiku is in the heart of the Central Highlands, which is supposed to be very scenic. This area is also inhabited by the Montagnard people who have a distinct culture of their own. They are also a different racial stock than the Vietnamese.[63] *Pleiku has also been very quiet the past few months. But the time passes quickly, it seems, in any case.*

I wrote a couple of letters to Gale Carman and Jerry Boice today.[64] *Gale's parents sent me a very nice Christmas card, enclosing a note with his address. He is with the 91st Evacuation Hospital, which is in Saigon. Boice is in an ambulance company in Pleiku. I heard from Hainzer when he first arrived in country, but I haven't received his address yet. I've also received no word from Hall at this point. So, I'm eager to hear from Boice and Carman and hear how they are getting along.*

Well, I better close for now. We haven't received any mail since we left Cu Chi. If you have written to me since the last part of December or first part of January, I haven't received anything... That's one of

---

[63] A hilltribe people of Vietnam, the Montagnard (a French term that means "mountain people) were often considered savages by other peoples of the region. However, they proved themselves to be courageous warriors and helped fight communists alongside the United States during the Vietnam War. In the years after the war, many Montagnard refugees were relocated to the U.S., many of whom were settled in North Carolina.

[64] Gale Carman graduated from high school in Paris, Missouri, in 1965. He completed his tour with the 91st Evacuation Hospital in Vietnam in early October 1968 and shortly thereafter was married to the former Barbara Kay Rives of the Moberly, Missouri area. The September 19, 1968 edition of the *Moberly Monitor-Index.* In the years after the war, Carman moved to the Columbia, Missouri, area and went on to complete a four-decade career with the United States Postal Service. Jerry Boice continued his education after the war and rose through several levels of school administration in Illinois, eventually becoming a superintendent before retiring.

*the problems of moving around: the mail gets back-
logged, but they have assured us that it is on the way.
Say hi to everyone for me and write when you can.*

Roger

* * *

Buchta goes on to cite in his previous letter several of the friends
he trained with back in the states who were now also serving in various locations in Vietnam. These friends included Gale Carman, Jerry
Boice, Alan Hall, and Dennis Hainzer.

"Roger and I entered the service about the same time and did
our basic together at Ft. Hood, followed by our AIT at Ft. Sam
Houston, and then our assignment with an ambulance company at
Ft. Hood," Carman recalled. "After that, he deployed to Vietnam
about the same time. We always got along well, and I can remember
while we were still in Texas, I took the top bunk, and he took the
lower bunk because, for some reason, he was not comfortable with
sleeping on the top bunk."

He continued, "There were a few of us, including Roger, who
would hang out and go to the movies on the weekends, among other
things. Roger was always sort of the quiet type, but he could be very
funny at times."

Carman remarked that when he and Buchta deployed to
Vietnam, his friend was sent closer to the action, near the DMZ.
However, he was assigned to the 91st Evacuation Hospital, which
was, at the time, located near a town called Tuy Hoa. Both he and
Buchta, Carman explained, returned from Vietnam and received

their discharges from the Army around the same timeframe. In later years the two were able to reconnect, albeit briefly.

"There was a time a few years after the war when Roger and Jerry Boice were able to come up to my house near Columbia for one weekend," Carman recalled. "I think that may have been the only time we got together after the war." He added, "I was sure saddened to hear of his passing, because Roger was a great guy, and I always knew he would have my back."

Jerry Boice, who is also mentioned in Buchta's letter, was part of the coterie of friends that included Buchta, Carman, and Denny Hainzer.

"I was Roger's platoon leader in basic training, and we went through medic training at Ft. Sam Houston together. I can tell you that he was a good soldier, and he did what he had to do. He spoke German, which I found interesting, and he was probably smarter than any professors he ever had in college." Pausing, he went on to discuss his friend's dedication to his military responsibilities: "We were among a group of guys that were drafted, but everybody tried to do their fair share, and he was no exception to that. Roger was fun to be around, and, although he may not have done any heroics that I know about, he was a good man."

Both Carman and Boice affirmed that as the years passed, they lost contact with Dennis Hainzer, who also deployed to Vietnam around the same time as the rest of the group of friends. Assigned to the 4th Infantry Division, Hainzer was wounded two weeks following his arrival in Vietnam, and he lost one of his legs as a result.

In his previous letter, Buchta also took the time, to explain in rather elaborate detail, the hospital layout in Lai Khe. The Office of Medical History of the U.S. Army Medical Department reported, "(s)emi-permanent, air-conditioned, fully equipped hospitals were constructed at a number of (base) camps" and were not designed to "follow the advancing army in direct support of tactical operations." Instead, these hospitals, such as the ones where Buchta served, often became fixed installations that relied primarily upon air evacuation to bring casualties to their landing zones, and from there relied upon ambulances to get them to a specific treatment location on the base. The report further revealed: "Electrical power was limited in the cities and lacking in the countryside. Generators were installed to provide the vast quantities of current needed for lighting, air-conditioning units, and the electrically powered equipment of a modern hospital. Water was equally limited. Wells were dug or water piped in to furnish the running water needed for bathing, laundry, sterilization of equipment, and operation of flush toilets."[65]

One of the early companies contracted by the Department of Defense to design and produce the Medical Unit Self Contained Transportable (MUST) hospitals for the Army Medical Service was the Air Cruisers Divisions of the Garrett Corporation of New Jersey. The company was awarded a $5,635,500 contract in early January 1968 "for fabrication of inflatable shelters," although the first prototype had been demonstrated back in 1965, and earlier models of the MUST hospital were already being used in Vietnam. As part of the contract, the Garrett Corporation's AiRearch Manufacturing Division produced the utility support packages for the hospital,

---

[65] Medical Support of the U.S. Army in Vietnam, *Hospitalization and Evacuation*, 59-65.

including electrical and pneumatic power units, hot and cold water, air-conditioning and heating.[66]

The 18th Surgical Hospital, which Buchta explained did not provide a glowing welcome to the soldiers of the 542nd Medical Company because of their frenetic schedules, possessed a lineage dating back to their formation in December 1928. The hospital served in the Pacific theater during World War II and was deactivated in 1945, in the weeks following the war's end. However, they were reorganized, and activated in 1963, and they received credit for serving in several campaigns of the Vietnam War, earning two Meritorious Unit Commendations. Several months prior to Buchta's arrival in Lai Khe, the 18th Surgical Hospital had provided medical support from the base in Pleiku—the same location where Buchta had expressed in his previous letter that he would like to visit. A Department of Army report dated August 15, 1966, stated, "The 18th Surgical Hospital (MA) is composed of 91 enlisted men and 31 officers and has the mission of performing basic resuscitative surgery and emergency life-saving measures in preparing patients for further evacuation to the rear." The report further details the composite of the hospital as having the major section of "Pre-Operative, Surgery, Post-Operative, Holding, Pharmacy, Laboratory and X-Ray, Admission and Disposition, and Central Material Supply, plus its administrative sections." [67]

* * *

---

[66] January 21, 1968 edition of the *Asbury Park Press*.
[67] Department of the Army, *Operational Report for Quarterly Period*, 1.

Sp/4. Roger Buchta
542nd Medical Company
Lai Khe, South Vietnam
January 21, 1968

Dear Mom, Dad and Don:

Well, another month has just about passed into history. At the end of the month, I will have been in Vietnam four months. It really hasn't seemed that long. It is really strange how one so completely loses all conception of time. One day I'll check the date; the next time I check, three or four days will have elapsed, and I can't explain to myself where they went. In Vietnam, there is no weekend or even day or night. The war respects no time. Of course, when one finds out the day he leaves for the states, time takes on a new meaning; then time is all-important. My time is coming, hopefully in July or August.

We have been putting in a full day's work this past week. The personnel of the 18th Surgical Hospital have been doing some building in their area. As a result, we have resumed many of their duties in the hospital. We work six days a week, twelve hours a day. I have been working the night shift. It really isn't hard work, but the hours drag by. I really can't seem to get used to the routine. During the day, it's so hot that it is sometimes difficult to get a good eight hours of sleep. This week, however, we are going back on eight-hour shifts. There certainly wasn't any argument over this, at least from the men of the 542nd.

There was a rumor that the 542nd might be converted into a surgical hospital on a miniature scale. This idea has cooled somewhat. After considering the tremendous expense and potential, the big brass is deciding that it is not practical for a unit as small as ours. But, of course, nothing has been decided. None of us are enthusiastic over the idea because of the tremendous work that is involved and the type of patients that we'll have to deal with. In a surgical hospital, you deal with casualties directly from the field aid stations who require emergency surgery. After recovering from the operation, the casualties are evacuated to larger hospitals. Some of the more serious cases are sent to Japan and back to the states. So, it is hard work dealing with these types of patients. About 90% of the casualties who arrive here never return to the field. One of the first things they say as the anesthetic wears off is: "Doc, am I going back? They can't make me. I will be sent back to the states, won't I?" It is sometimes a pathetic sight, but LBJ's fight to bring "democracy" to 'Nam continues.

We are supposed to leave in another two or three weeks. The destination will probably be back to Qui Nhon before going elsewhere. Like in my last letter, that's about all I know at this point.

The last letter that I've received from you was dated January 2nd. Our mail has really been fouled up due to the moving around. I was interested to hear that you have begun decorating the dining room. When you are through, I want you to send me a snapshot of it...

Better close for now and get a little shuteye. Stay well and write soon.

Roger

* * *

The soldier appears to be experiencing a period of calm in his duties with the hospital, not realizing the storm that is soon to be unleashed. Within nine days from the date of his previous letter, the first phase of the assaults in the Tet Offensive would be launched by enemy forces, involving coordinated surprise attacks by an estimated 70,000-80,000 North Vietnamese and Viet Cong against U.S. and South Vietnamese forces. There would be heavy casualties inflicted on both sides and, although the United States would, in the end, succeed in repelling the attacks and regain lost ground, this offensive became a major turning point in the war. This offensive helped the American public realize that the war was far from being over, and their support for the war quickly evaporated. The Tet Offensive would become one of the primary factors leading to the U.S. withdrawal from Vietnam a few years later. Many infantry units would be enmeshed in combat operations to repel the assaults by enemy forces, resulting in multiple casualties to be treated by medical facilities throughout Vietnam, including the 18th Surgical Hospital at Lai Khe.

* * *

Sp/4. Roger Buchta
542nd Medical Company
Lai Khe, South Vietnam
January 23, 1968

Dear Mom, Dad and Don:

Today I received your letter and the booklet that I requested from Don. I was very glad to have received a letter from you and hope that you will continue writing during those long, cold winter nights. Don writes very interesting letters, but I would like to hear what you and Dad have to say, also.

Well, not much has happened since I wrote you last. Today and tomorrow, I have off. My time has been spent just lying around, reading, and occasionally going to the icebox for a soda. Some of us guys chipped in and bought an icebox at the PX. It is not very large—about four feet high, but it serves our purposes well. It is a Japanese brand. It cost each of us $10.00. When one of us leaves, we just sell our share to someone else. It is common practice in Vietnam. Each of us takes turns keeping it clean. We have a cook in the group who keeps it well stocked with leftovers from the mess hall. We also make a lot *of Kool-Aid and iced tea, which is necessary in this hot climate. Sometimes a fellow in the group will find some instant pudding. He makes some and puts it in the icebox with a sign saying, "Hands Off." He quickly finds many friends.*

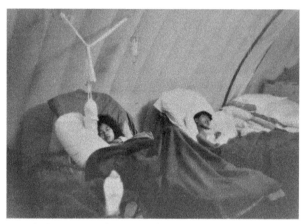

While stationed at Lai Khe, Buchta occasionally worked in a ward of the hospital that was dedicated to treating Vietnamese women and children who were wounded or injured because of hostile actions in the region.

Perhaps I can tell you a little bit about our living quarters here. We are living in a huge tent. It must be at least 70 feet by 30 feet. Before we pitched the tent, we built wooden floors and racks to hang our things on. We sleep on cots. Some of us, including myself, bought mattresses from a Vietnamese store. Almost all of us also purchased lawn chairs. Some of the more industrious guys made tables and desks. All of this may sound very crude, but it really isn't. We also have plenty of shade from huge rubber trees. The NCOs and Sp/5s also have two small tents of their own. Every Saturday night, we have a hootenanny in the NCO tent. The unit is allotted so much money for recreation, which usually means cases and cases of beer every Saturday night. Of course, with all the beer the guys just get to feeling good and that's about all. Our two group leaders, who are both doctors, usually drop in and take part. They sure are swell fellows. Both of them were drafted for two years just like me; as the result, they have the same interests and expectations as most of us draftees do. They really look out after our interests.

When we first arrived, we couldn't get any linen from the unit that we are supporting. As soon as the two men found out about it, they got together with the sergeants and got us some linens. Our "bosses" at the hospital don't dare get on us for anything, because they know if they do, our two doctors will be down on their you-know-what. Each man in the unit knows the kind of leaders we have; as a result, there is very good cooperation and no discipline problems. Our unit is very small resulting in close relationships with one another. We all call each other by our first names. You really don't realize how much all of this means, especially here in 'Nam. It sure makes our situation more pleasant.

As I began saying, each Saturday we have a jam session. Three fellows have guitars. We have one Mexican from Texas who can really play. Last Saturday they played country music. The Mexican got mixed up in the middle of a country song and gave the song a Mexican beat. It was really funny. One of the other fellows who plays is from Cameron, Missouri. He and a guy from St. Louis are the only men from Missouri except me. Next Saturday evening we are planning a touch football game and a barbecue. So, it should be a pretty enjoyable evening.

This week I have been working on the ward as usual. Believe it or not, my job was babysitting this week. There is one ward set aside for Vietnamese. Most of the patients are children and women who were injured as a result of hostile action. They are brought here for emergency surgery and remain until they recover or until they are evacuated to a larger hospital. At present, we have about seven or eight patients, including a two-year-old girl who is recovering from a fragment wound. We also have two babies, one of which is only three weeks old. I have had to do everything from change diapers to burping the babies. I have one Vietnamese civilian woman to help me. It is a shame that I won't put my baby knowledge to good use. Guess I'll have to get married when I get home. Ha!...

That is about all the gossip I can pass along for now. In your letter you expressed some concern over our safety. If you are worrying about my safety, forget it! No matter where we go, or how we go, we'll always be well protected. The area we are in now is as safe as if we were camped down at the creek. We are a medical company, meaning that a safe area has to be provided before we can set up to operate. This is common sense. I am really safer over here than I was when I drove to and from school each day. Another point: don't take seriously all you hear and see on radio, TV, and in the papers. Much of it is exaggerated in order to create interest. Use the time you spend worrying about me caring for Grandma and for those who really need it. I'm a military man, that's an order! So long for now. Take care of yourself and write soon.

Roger

* * *

At the point of his previous letter, the beginning of the Tet Offensive was one week away. The medic attempted to stress to his mother not to worry about his safety, because he was stationed in an extremely safe location. As he revealed in later conversations with his brother, Buchta had no reason to disbelieve this, since, if there was any intelligence that existed regarding the coming assaults, it had not been shared with lower enlisted soldiers. Little did he realize, at the time, that the sheer number of forces would nearly overwhelm several U.S. bases in the coming days and create great cause for concern, even for those serving in a medical capacity. When the first stage of the Tet Offensive began to evolve on January 30 and 31, the primary focus of the attacks were against "mostly populated areas and places with heavy U.S. troop presence," noted an article by the Office of the Historian of the U.S. Department of State. "The strikes on the major cities of Hué and Saigon had a strong psychological impact, since they showed that the NLF (South Vietnamese National Liberation Forces) who supported the communist forces were not as weak as the Johnson Administration had previously claimed."[68] During the offensive, the NLF even managed to breach the outer walls of the U.S. Embassy in Saigon. Considering the location of Lai Khe, which was essentially on the outskirts of Saigon, Buchta would soon receive an unwanted view of the opening states of the Tet Offensive.

* * *

Sp/4. Roger Buchta
542nd Medical Company
Lai Khe, South Vietnam
January 30, 1968

Dear Mom, Dad and Don:

It's the end of another day in Vietnam. It's also the end of another month and payday. Payday is the GI's favorite day. Everybody carefully examines his pay voucher for new deductions, which are common. Then it's a rush to the post office for money orders. Obtaining a money order necessitates stand-

---

[68] U.S. Department of State, *U.S. Involvement in the Vietnam War*, <u>https://history.state.gov</u>.

ing in a long line for as long as an hour or more. It can be a very tedious job. It is really surprising sometimes to see just how much money everybody sends home. Most of the money that is sent home is used for a car when the individual leaves the service. Some fellows buy their cars over here and have them waiting when they return home. The cars are sold for wholesale directly from the manufacturer. You can get quite a savings. This fellow, Bailey, ordered himself a Dodge Charger last week. I plan to send home at least $250 in a week or so. This month I'll get full E-4 pay.

This week I am not working on the ward; instead, I'm working on bunkers and building sandbag walls around our tents. Each week one man leaves the hospital and helps the NCOs around the living area. We work about seven or eight hours a day. Mostly we BS and drive around the camp looking for things which we need but never find. It is just an excuse to go driving around. We have a first lieutenant who works with us, and he really works. He hates anything military and told me one day he works with us to pass the time. He's supposed to be an administrative officer with the unit, but he actually has no real job. Next week I'm supposed to work at the receiving and emergency area of the hospital. Here we take the casualties off the choppers and prepare them for surgery. It can be very interesting. The other day, one of our doctors performed an emer-

gency surgery [in the area] where the patients are received since the operating rooms were in use when the casualty came in. I watched the operation. The doctor removed wooden splinters from deep inside the casualty's face. The splinters were causing intracranial pressure (pressure on the brain). He opened up the whole side of the man's face. This was quite a task for this man, who is not a brain surgeon but an orthopedist. The splinters, however, were not causing as much damage as was anticipated. The operation under the conditions was really remarkable. We certainly gained more respect for this doctor, who is one of our two. Our two doctors are very skilled in their profession and about two of the most friendly and courteous men you could ever meet. We are very fortunate to have them in our unit. During mass operations in the field, when there are suddenly a large number of casualties, it isn't uncommon to see a doctor performing major surgery under a shade tree. No matter how badly a casualty is wounded, if he's alive when he arrives as the hospital, the chances are 98% of the time he can be saved. This fantastic percentage is completely unheard of in past conflicts. We really have to take our hats off to the Army Medical Service. Of course, there is no substitute for peace and a lack of casualties...

I got a couple of letters from my Ft. Hood buddies. Carman wrote me that he is with the 91st Evacuation Hospital at Saigon. He discussed his "tearful" departure from his girl when he left St. Louis. He said he plans to get married as soon as he is out of the service. He already gave me an informal wedding invitation. Isn't that great? Hainzer wrote me that he wasn't as fortunate as the rest of us. He is a combat medic with the 4th Infantry Division at Dak To. I sure hope everything goes well for him for he's a great guy. The rest of us could have easily been in his shoes, but we were fortunate…

Better close this gossip session and catch up on my reading a bit. Write soon and that includes all of you except the dogs, I guess. Stay well, be good, and all that.

Love,
Roger

* * *

Within hours of writing his previous letter to his family, the first phase of the Tet Offensive began. Although enemy operations blossomed to the point where it would appreciably impact the medical staff at Lai Khe, there appears to have been some notice to leadership at the base of the approaching enemy offensive. Buchta was assigned to assist several other soldiers in placing sandbags around their living area for protection in case of mortar attacks. The unsettling welcome of thunderous mortar explosions would soon greet those on the base in the early morning hours. Many of the soldiers mistakenly believed these explosions to be outgoing artillery rounds used to harass enemy troops.

Lou Pumphrey, who, like Buchta, was a U.S. Army draftee and specialist fourth class, was also serving at Lai Khe when the Tet Offensive launched in the early morning hours of January 31, 1968. Assigned to the Public Information Office of the First Infantry Division, Pumphrey recalled his "first experience with enemy rocket fire" when he "saw a bright flash of white light out of the corner of my right eye, followed by a loud explosion about 100 yards away."[69] Jolted from his bunk, he, and many of his fellow soldiers, sought protection by rushing for the safety of a nearby bunker.

Buchta experienced a similar response; however, seeking to allay his mother's fears for his safety, most of his letters reveal very little about the assault. In the years after the war, Roger would share, in confidence with his older brother, many of the details of his own experiences when the Tet Offensive unfolded at Lai Khe.

"He informed me that Viet Cong attempted to breach the perimeter of the base at Lai Khe, and the medical staff were ordered to get into a ditch that essentially surrounded the base," said Don Buchta. "They had their M-16 rifles, and all hell was breaking loose around them with a firefight going on and mortars exploding. Then, one of the sergeants hollered, 'Ok, men! Lock and load!'[70] With a pause, recollecting conversations from years past, his brother added, "Roger said it was one command that he would always remember. When all the firing finally ended, there were about thirty Viet Cong

---

[69] Millner, *The Tet Offensive*, https://cleveland.com
[70] "Lock and load" is a phrase used to describe the process of locking the magazine or cartridge into the chamber of a rifle in preparation to fire the weapon.

that had been killed, but Roger didn't think the U.S. suffered any casualties."

Official military reports indicate that, by the time the Tet Offensive ended, the base camp at Lai Khe endured more than 980 rocket and mortar rounds. The base camp had been well protected by the gallant soldiers of the First Infantry Division who, in the weeks prior to the assault, had been engaged in activities that included conducting road security operations and base camp security sweeps. During the offensive, the soldiers of the "Big Red One" would carry the fight to the enemy and, several months later, even lost the division commanding general, Major General Keith L. Ware, and his aides when enemy forces shot down their helicopter near Loc Ninh on September 13, 1968.[71]

* * *

Sp/4. Roger Buchta
542nd Medical Company
Lai Khe, South Vietnam
February 2, 1968

Dear Mom, Dad and Don:
It's another hot Vietnam-type afternoon. The temperatures must be near, or over, the 100-degree mark. The huge rubber trees over our camp provide quite a bit of shade. With the lack of any breeze, though, the heat seems to hit you in monstrous waves.

---

[71] First Division Museum at Cantigny Park, *Vietnam*, https://fdmuseum.org.

During the day, we roll up the sides of the tent and strip down to our shorts. The icebox is also kept well stocked with soda, Kool-Aid, and beer. As soon as the sun goes down, there is a noticeable change; in fact, you often have to cover with a blanket or two. The monsoons in this area of Vietnam don't come around until September or October, which means no rain until then. The dust is really hell. When a helicopter takes off or lands, it produces such a cloud of dust that you lose sight of it until its high in the air. But I suppose there have been very few wars fought under ideal climatic conditions.

This week has been a very easy week from the standpoint of work. I was supposed to be working in the living area doing various odd jobs that needed to be done. We finished what had to be done Tuesday. The rest of the week we just sat around reading, writing, and BS'ing. We also had a few alerts this week. As you undoubtedly heard in the news, the VC and NVA have been kicking up their heels a bit. They have a strange way of celebrating their new year. I can't understand sometimes how these people can absorb the tremendous losses that they suffer and still continue fighting. Many people feel that this last drive by the communists was their last. But, of course, they have said this many times before, but the war seems to drag on. I doubt if there will be any real change until elections. Although we were on alert a few times, nothing developed in this area.

Most of the enemy activity seemed to be centered in the area where there is huge concentration of civilians and troops. They also have a great desire to lob a few mortars on airstrips now and then. The activity has slowed down considerably.

Next week I'll be working in the receiving area of the hospital. Here, as I may have mentioned in my last letter, we take the casualties off the helicopters and prepare them for surgery. This preparation involves removing the clothes, dressings, and splints. Then it's necessary to clean and disinfect the site where surgery will be performed. The casualties' vital signs are taken, records assembled, and then he's taken to the X-Ray lab if time is available. From the lab, he'll go to surgery. It usually takes about ten minutes after the casualty arrives 'til he goes to the operating room. I'll learn more about the procedure after I begin working there.

I was surprised to hear that the letter I sent to KLIK was read on the air. One night, I was "feeling pretty good" with a little time on my hands. While listening to the radio, I thought it might kill a little time if I wrote KLIK and informed the staff that the station here at Lai Khe has the same call letters as the station back home in [Jefferson City]. I had no idea it would be taken seriously.

The last letter which I received from you was dated January 20th. The mail situation is really screwed up in this area. It is brought here from Saigon by convoy. As a result, it is often delayed due to people who simply don't give a damn whether it's delivered promptly or not. They only bring mail every three or four days. Then it has to be sorted and delivered to the various units. I don't know if the situation is due to inefficiency or just that it can't be delivered quicker...

That's about all I can think of for now. I sure wish some of the heat here in 'Nam could be sent back to the states. But I guess spring is not far off. Then it will be the same old story—gardening, repairing, and catfishing. Hope you all are well. Write soon.

Roger

Shortly after the kickoff of the Tet Offensive, Buchta explained that the 18th Surgical Hospital began to disassemble one of their portable hospitals in the event it had to be moved further into the interior of the base of Lai Khe to prevent damage from rocket and mortar attacks.

The tense opening moments of what would become known as the Tet Offensive began to subside in the following days. From Buchta's perspective, operating from the insulated interior areas of the base camp, he was privy to many of the defensive and offensive operations that were taken by the soldiers of the First Infantry Division in the coming weeks. His observations, regarding the attack and the aftermath, were very intuitive. Roger noted that airfields and locations with concentrations of both troops and civilians appeared to be prime targets for enemy offensives.

"Political cadres accompanied the assault groups with the intent, in vain as it turned out, to coax the local population into rebellion," wrote Andrew J. Trass in the U.S. Army's Center of Military History publication *U.S. Army Campaigns of the Vietnam War: Turning Point, 1967-1968*." He added, "The fighting in Hue and Saigon was especially vicious, and throughout the country heavy rocket, and mortar fire, and demolition charges damaged airfields, logistical facilities, and supply routes. While the South Vietnamese government and its forces constituted the prime enemy target, U.S. units were swept into the turmoil."[72]

As in previous letters, the medic sought to avoid alarming his mother with regard to his own exposure to rocket and mortar attacks; instead, he shared vague statements regarding the overall circumstances of the offensive, and he quickly transitioned to lighter subjects, such as the letter he had written to his local radio station back in Jefferson City, Missouri. The *Sunday News Tribune* reported on January 21, 1968, one of the local radio stations had received a letter from Buchta stating, "In Lai Khe, where I am presently stationed,

---

[72] Trass, *U.S. Army Campaigns of the Vietnam War*, 49.

the Armed Forces Radio Station is known as KLIK... It was a surprise when I first listened to this station and heard station identification." His letter continued, "For a moment I thought I was back home. But the sound of helicopters overhead, and the almost constant roar of artillery, told me this was not so. Nevertheless, it is still good to hear station KLIK, even though it is not in Jefferson City, but more than 10,000 miles away." KLIK is a news and talk radio station that continues to serve the central Missouri area. The KLIK station that Buchta mentioned listening to in Vietnam was an Armed Forces Radio Network Vietnam (AFVN), which was also referred to as "Radio Lai Khe" and was initially operated by First Brigade of the First Division but was later moved to the Public Information Office of the division.[73]

* * *

Sp/4. Roger Buchta
542nd Medical Company
Lai Khe, South Vietnam
February 5, 1968

Dear Mom, Dad and Don:
I am dropping you a few lines to accompany the money orders, which are enclosed. We got paid a few days ago, although we only received partial pay. Our pay records weren't sent here from Cu Chi. So,

---

[73] Armed Forces Vietnam Network Memories, *KLIK—The "Big Red One,"* https://afvnvets.net.

they did manage to get us partial pay. As soon as we receive the remainder of January's pay, I'll send some more money home.

As you undoubtedly heard in the news, there has been quite a bit of communist activity in Vietnam the last week or so. There were rumors that the enemy was planning a ground attack on Lai Khe. As a result, the 18th Surgical and the 542nd have been on alert to retreat to the center of the camp in the event of a ground attack. But nothing has developed. The 18th had disassembled part of their $7,000,000 hospital in preparation of moving it in case of an attack. About all we have done is just sit around. Everything seems to be returning to normal.

Saturday night we were supposed to have a barbecue, but due to this alert, it was a pretty quiet evening. We drank a few beers, listened to the Grand Ol' Opry, and hit the sack. Tex Ritter was the emcee. His performance was somewhat cleaner than at the Lake.[74] We also listened to Gunsmoke, which is on the radio, and the characters are unknowns. The last time I heard a radio show like this was about fifteen

---

[74] Tex Ritter was a country music performer, radio show host and actor born near the southwest Missouri community of Carthage. In his letter, Buchta refers to the Lake of Ozarks, where Tex Ritter and other musical stars of the period often performed at such venues as the former Austin Wood Auditorium.

years ago when we listened to the Sergeant Preston Show.[75]

That's about all for now…

Roger

* * *

Buchta now reveals to his family that a major offensive has begun in Vietnam, but remains circumspect when describing the actual impact recent events have had on himself and fellow medical personnel serving at the base. Although the situation has returned to a level of relative normalcy when compared to activity in previous weeks, Roger does imply that further attacks are suspected. He also remarks that the 18th Surgical Hospital has begun preparations to move to a safer location further to the interior of the base as a precaution.

Despite the stresses caused by the initial assault in the Tet Offensive, the soldier does seem to enjoy the welcome lull by embracing the opportunity to enjoy a few drinks in his tent while listening to radio programs that remind him of past days back in Missouri. The silence at Lai Khe, though unknown to Buchta at the time, is only a temporary reprieve. However, many locations throughout the country continue to suffer attacks while the offensive progresses. This reality will soon result in an increased casualty load for the medical

---

[75] Here refers to "Sergeant Preston of the Yukon," a radio adventure series that became the television series of the same name in 1955.

staff and lead to long hours and exposure to a variety of wounds in the coming weeks, as infantry units throughout Vietnam continue battling the North Vietnamese and Viet Cong forces.

CHAPTER 6

Shadows of War Lengthen

There is a rumor on the grapevine that the 542nd [Medical Company] and the 18th [Surgical Hospital] will be moving to a new site soon. In fact, the hospital is on alert to move in seventy-two hours if the order comes to move... The 18th came to Lai Khe in December [1967]. I can't see why they would move so soon after arriving here." –Buchta in a letter he wrote home in mid-February 1968.

When entering the second week of February 1968, a little more than a week after the opening stages of the Tet Offensive, Buchta disclosed in his writings that despite rumors that North Vietnam was planning a full-scale invasion of South Vietnam, things had become rather quiet at Lai Khe. Within the first week of Tet, Buchta explained, the Communist forces lost 15,000 fighters while the loss of American lives was negligible. Although the information Buchta was receiving was likely being vetted and filtered through such sources as Armed Forces Radio and military newspapers, the *New York Times* reported on January 31, 1988, on the twentieth anniversary of the attack, that "[b]y mid-February, or two weeks into the offensive, Washington was estimating that enemy casualties had risen to almost 39,000, including 33,249 killed. Allied casualties were placed at 3,470 dead, one-third of them Americans..."[76]

The attack created such a heightened state of vigilance, by U.S. forces at Lai Khe, that the 18th Surgical Hospital evacuated patients in expectation that they would soon be receiving mass casualties. After a few days, the anticipated casualties did not arrive. Buchta noted that the majority of them had been sent to medical facilities located a Long Binh or Saigon. The few casualties the hospital did end up receiving, he added, were evacuated following any surgical procedures because of concerns of mortar and rocket attacks in the area. The medic shared that his duty, working in the receiving and evacuation hospital, had been relatively quiet for the past several days since they seldom received more than "one or two patients at the most" during his shifts.

---

[76] January 31, 1988 edition of the *New York Times*.

Mirroring many of his earlier letters, Buchta did point out one of the most demoralizing circumstances on Lai Khe that resulted from the Tet Offensive—the Post Exchange had been closed for several days because merchandise had not been received. The interruptions in the supply network not only impacted the soldiers who were now unable to purchase assorted comfort items they had come to appreciate, but also resulted in the depletion of critical medical provisions at the hospital. To work around the transportation challenges, Buchta's platoon was able to dispatch two soldiers to Long Binh aboard a helicopter to acquire the needed medical supplies. In addition to the required medical supplies, the soldiers returned with two items that gained them renewed popularity among their fellow soldiers—cigarettes and booze. Additionally, the duo returned with batteries, since a generator on base had been blown up two weeks earlier, likely in a mortar attack, creating a significant increase in usage and desire for flashlights that used the batteries.

In his writings, Buchta also found time to provide more detailed descriptions and observations regarding the layout of Lai Khe. The medic revealed something of a fascination with the rubber trees that grew on and around the base, which, upon his arrival, appeared to be completely bare, resembling "giant tinker-toys stuck in the ground." As the weeks passed, the trees began to take on varying shades of green. Roger discovered, while watching other soldiers around the base, that if a sharp object was stuck in the tree sap would gush from the incision in the bark. Initially, he explained, the sap resembled a sort of cream but, within a day or so, began to harden and acquire an elasticity. There were also opportunities for Roger to observe, with rapt amazement, the Vietnamese workers who tapped the rubber trees during the harvest, stripping back the bark and using knives to cut a groove to collect the "latex." The studious soldier also learned that the area surrounding the base was once part an area developed by the French as the 31,000-acre Michelin Rubber Plantation. At the time of Buchta's service in Lai Khe, the plantation was owned by the Vietnamese government, and the trees were considered so valuable that any time one was destroyed by U.S. forces, the Vietnamese government was provided a restitution of eighty-five dollars for each damaged tree.

* * *

While stationed at Lai Khe, Buchta observed with fascination the process used to harvest "latex" from rubber trees on the Michelin Rubber Plantation surrounding the base.

Sp/4. Roger Buchta
542nd Medical Company
Lai Khe, South Vietnam
February 19, 1968

Dear Mom, Dad and Don:

Another week has come and gone. It was an unusually quiet week compared to the couple weeks before and after Tet. Everything is beginning to return to normal. There is still a little activity in the Saigon area, but things seem to be settling down. The big trouble spot now is near the DMZ at Khe San. The NVA is supposed to have control of the area surrounding the city. But the Marines are there. You've probably heard, in the news, where the Air Reserve is being reactivated. The draft calls in the next few months are supposed to be quite high. The February and March draftees, or one of these draftees I should say, will be my replacement. Isn't that nice? Of course, the Korean situation has had a lot to do with reactivating the reserves and increasing the draft.[77]

Work at the hospital has been proceeding as usual, with one exception: we are now on eight-hour shifts. No one seemed to object to this. This new change now provides us ample time for outside interests, such

---

[77] This remark is in connection to the USS Pueblo—a U.S. Navy intelligence vessel that was attacked and captured by North Korean forces on January 23, 1968. The eighty-two U.S. crewmen who survived the incident were released eleven months later.

as reading and writing. Other than those two, there is very little to occupy oneself. They are trying to get some horseshoe sets and some volleyball equipment. It would be nice to have some means of killing our free time. There is a rumor on the grapevine that the 542nd and the 18th Surgical will be moving to a new site soon. In fact, the hospital is on alert to move out in seventy-two hours if the order comes down to move. I don't see how the hospital could move in seventy-two hours. A week and a half is more like it. I haven't heard anything in the past few days, so maybe it is all blowing over. The 18th first came down to Lai Khe in December; I can't see why they would move so soon after arriving here. Before coming down here, they were in Pleiku. The 542nd was also attached to them there, before it went back to the home base in Qui Nhon. The unit was reformed and is once again with the 18th Surgical Hospital. The 542nd won't get a replacement unit until it leaves to return to the home base. If we remained attached to the 18th as long as we are supposed to, I and about half a dozen others will leave the 18th and Vietnam about the same time. At first, we were dismayed when we learned that we would be attached to the 18th. This was mainly because of the type of patients with which we would have to deal. Ordinarily, we would only care for casualties with minor wounds or illnesses, but now, since each man has learned the procedures, many are beginning to like it. They are working out a rotation program, whereby members of our platoon can rotate with men in other platoons back at Qui Nhon on a voluntary basis. Our platoon leader, who was at Qui Nhon recently, said the men back there are begging to have a chance of coming to Lai Khe. Qui Nhon is almost like a base in the states. They have inspections and almost every kind of harassment that exists back home. Discipline is as bad as it was back at Ft. Hood. Here at Lai Khe, each man is virtually on his own. There is a much more relaxed atmosphere. Of course, it is much more primitive than at Qui Nhon, but it doesn't take long to become accustomed to the difference in living conditions... I've learned quite a bit with the 18th. I know what my job is and would prefer to stay where I am. The men in the 18th have been very cooperative, and I've become acquainted with them...

...[I]t was somewhat of a surprise to hear McKee got the axe and was replaced by Snead.[78] It was an interesting note about Terry Kruse from Russellville. I was wondering what his classification is. I read in the paper where Lincoln [University] will increase the number of games they play next year.

---

[78] Buchta is referencing Grover Snead, who was hired in 1968 to serve as superintendent of Russellville (Missouri) schools. A native of Harrison County, Missouri, Snead was serving as superintendent of schools in Jamestown, Missouri when he accepted the job in nearby Russellville. Paul McKee, who is also referenced in the letter, was the previous superintendent for Russellville schools. August 11, 1968 edition of the *Sunday News and Tribune*.

I may have to go to a few games and check this Kruse kid out. I can imagine the publicity he got [79] *…*

That's about all the gossip I can think of for now. Hope all of you are well and enjoying all those cold February days. Write soon.

Roger

* * *

At Lai Khe, Buchta and a majority of his fellow enlisted soldiers lived in large tents such as the one pictured here. They erected the tents on wooden floors and had such amenities as a small refrigerator in which to keep soda and beer.

---

[79] At the time of Buchta's letter, Terry Kruse was married to the former Nancy Wyss of Russellville and a junior attending Lincoln University in Jefferson City. A former all-stater from Selden, Kansas, he became a star player of the Lincoln University basketball team, the Blue Tigers. February 11, 1968 edition of the *Sunday News and Tribune*.

The effects of the Tet Offensive may have cooled to a limited extent at Lai Khe, Buchta explained, but battles continued to rage in areas such as Saigon and by the Marines Corps at Khe Shan. The Battle of Khe Shan, history demonstrates, began on January 21, 1968, when "around 20,000 men from the North Vietnamese Army (fought) against some 6,000 US Marines and South Vietnamese Army soldiers." The battle would last seventy-seven days and grow to involve more than 45,000 U.S. soldiers and as many as 100,000 North Vietnamese (NVA) troops. Speculation exists as to the number of casualties that resulted from the fighting, but estimates range from 1,000 to 3,500 US soldiers who died, "and a secret report from the US Military Assistance Command, Vietnam, estimated that only 5,500 NVA troops were killed."[80]

Mention of the draftees that will be coming into the military in the next several weeks highlights Buchta's eye for the future, as he knows the wheels of the system continue to spin toward bringing his replacement into Vietnam. It may not have been as "busy" as previous years, but 1968 resulted in the induction of 296,406 young men into the U.S. military through the Selective Service System, or what is more commonly known as the military draft. Buchta recognized that these new draftees were not only needed for the war raging in Vietnam, but they were also needed to support the "Korean situation." The situation he mentions in his letter occurred on January 23, 1968, only a few days before the height of the Tet Offensive. The USS *Pueblo*—a U.S. Navy light cargo ship—was confronted during surveillance of the North Korean coast while in international waters and was subsequently captured by North Korean torpedo boats. "The 82

---

[80] Brimelow, *50 Years Ago*, https://businessinsider.com.

Pueblo survivors endured 11 months of cruel captivity before being released on 23 December 1968."[81] The entire incident nearly created a scenario that led to a second war with North Korea.

The discussions he embarks upon in his letter then swing to his continuing work with the 18th Surgical Hospital, unveiling his appreciation for what he is learning during his daily duties and the medical staff with whom he works. He also affirms his desire to remain at Lai Khe rather than investigating the potential of transferring to the less "primitive" military base at Qui Nhon. Additionally, discussions of events related to both his alma maters—Russellville High School and Lincoln University—become a topic of "gossip" in the latter part of his letter and help keep him connected to communities back home.

* * *

Sp/4. Roger Buchta
542nd Medical Company
Lai Khe, South Vietnam
February 26, 1968

Dear Mom, Dad and Don:
It is a quiet, peaceful evening here in Lai Khe. About the only sound one can hear is the constant hum of the generator, which is started in the evening. Occasionally, a helicopter flies overhead. Other than those few sounds, it is very quiet. Actually, it has been

<hr>

[81] Naval History and Heritage Command, *Pueblo (AGER-2)*, https://history.navy.mil.

that way for the last week or so. We have only been admitting not more than a half-dozen people a day to the hospital, and most of those are civilians or South Vietnamese troops. Last night, for instance, a copter brought in a little boy and his mother, who had several fragment wounds. The boy also had several wounds, but they were only superficial. His mother, though, didn't fare so well. She had deep wounds in the stomach and bladder. They feared she wouldn't last through the operation, but she did, and, I understand, she's doing well today. Probably the worst cases we get are small children, especially babies. They must be watched continually once they return from surgery. They generally have a woman come in and babysit until the child is evacuated. It's really a funny war sometimes. You never know what you are going to see next.

The 18th and 542nd were on alert to move out, but nothing has happened, which suggests that we might not move. In fact, the rumor is that it has been called off. No one is too enthusiastic about moving, especially since we are finally settled down. Of course, we are also on eight-hour shifts now, which is also nice. Moving involves a lot of work, as you might imagine. They figure that it would take at least a month and a half from the time we left until we would be operational again in the new area. The hospital will move eventually, probably within the next two months for sure. But I do hope we stay here at least that long, since we are finally settled down.

Another fellow and I are discussing R&R plans at the present time. In some cases, they allow two men to go to the same place at the same time. We are going to try to go together. We were considering Australia until we discovered that one must be in-country at least ten months before he is eligible. It is easier to go to some places than others, because the Army has set a quota of the number of men who can go to certain places. Now we are thinking about either Hong Kong or Taipei. I kind of lean toward Taipei. Taipei is, of course, the capital of nationalist China. It is a very scenic island from the standpoint of historical sites and landscapes. It is also inexpensive to vacation there. But, of course, these plans are very tentative. If we go, we decided it would first be in July or the first part of August.

I have been keeping up with pro and college basketball. The other night there was about a five-minute sports editorial on this great star at LSU, Pete Maravich.[82] He must really be some shooter. He may be another Rick Barry on Bill Bradley, especially considering the fact that he is only a sophomore.[83] Forty-five points a game is some

---

[82] Often referred to as "Pistol Pete," Pete Maravich was a star player at LSU before becoming a first-round pick in 1970 for the Atlanta Hawks in the NBA draft. His professional basketball came to an end in 1980 because of severe knee problems. Maravich died from a heart attack in 1988 when playing a pickup basketball game in Pasadena, California.

[83] Rick Barry played basketball for the University of Miami and was drafted into the NBA in 1965, playing professional basketball until 1980. Bill Bradley

average. He may break every record in the book. I've been keeping up with Bradley, although he has been somewhat disappointing so far. But I suppose it takes time to get accustomed to pro ball. He should come through next year. And, of course, Jerry West has been burning the nets as usual...

That's about all I can think of for now. Stay well and write soon.

Roger

* * *

While stationed at Lai Khe, Buchta enjoyed taking numerous candid photographs and slides of several of the soldiers with whom he served in the 542nd Medical Company and 18th Surgical Hospital.

---

played for Princeton University and joined the New York Knicks for the 1967-1968 season. He played professional basketball until 1977 and went on to enter politics, becoming a United States Senator in 1978.

Rest and Recuperation, which the troops referred to as R&R, provided those completing their tours of a certain length in Vietnam, a break from their duties. A fairly detailed essay on "Tour of Duty" notes that a soldier was eligible for one R&R during their one-year tour of duty in country. There were several R&R locations approved by the military, including Taipei, which Buchta expressed an interest in visiting. Once a soldier was approved for his R&R leave, he was not allowed to carry any military clothing on his trip. Soldiers turned in their weapons and some of their other military gear, and, once they reached their destination, "rented" civilian clothing to be worn during their rest period. Individuals on R&R were subject to local laws and authorities, and, if they missed their return flight to their duty station, were considered to be "Absent without leave," or AWOL.[84]

In his letter, Buchta expresses an interest in basketball happenings back in the United States. Don Buchta recalls that, although his older brother often did not himself participate in sports, their family enjoyed attending many basketball games at Russellville High School in the late 1950s and early 1960s, at a time when the school was on a significant winning streak.

One particular item of interest, that does not weave its way into the Army medic's detailed letters home, pertains to a unique mascot that had been adopted by the soldiers of the 542nd—a massive python.

"Roger talked quite a bit about the python and said it took four guys to hold it," said Don Buchta. "Some of the soldiers there at Lai Khe purchased the snake from a local Vietnamese farmer and named it 'Pete,' and it essentially became their pet." He continued, "Apparently,

---

[84] Tour of Duty Advisor, *R&R and Leave in Vietnam,* https://tourofdutyinfo.com.

they had a large cage or crate that they kept Pete in, but one evening someone left it open and by the next morning, he had disappeared off into the rubber plantation, never to be seen again. At one time there were pictures of the guys holding Pete that Roger took while he was in Vietnam, but they disappeared somewhere down the line."

* * *

Sp/4. Roger Buchta
542nd Medical Company
Lai Khe, South Vietnam
March 5, 1968

Dear Mom, Dad and Don:

Well, another month has come, March—the windy month. It is the month that carries the last signs of winter and promises the coming of spring, which is right around the corner. It is the time when ball games are over and baseball players are beginning to think about and prepare themselves for the coming season. It seems that every month has some kind of character all its own. March in Vietnam this year will be a busy month for us. We received word last week that the 18th Surgical will be moving.

The announcement that we would be moving again came somewhat unexpectedly. Last Monday the hospital evacuated all its patients and quit receiving new ones. That same day we began disassembling the units and packing supplies. On

Wednesday we were finishing getting ready to move when they announced that departure would be delayed. Since Wednesday we have done nothing but sit around reading and playing cards. Nobody is objecting to the delay, but it is getting monotonous just sitting around. The hospital will leave Lai Khe by air. It will take forty planes to transport us to our new location, which is Da Nang. Da Nang is in the northern part of Vietnam, on the coast. It is one of the major supply centers in Vietnam and a R&R center for Marines. From all indications, it shouldn't be too bad. Da Nang is also in the coastal highlands, which means it should be cooler there. The plane trip will take about four hours. That's really all I know about the situation at this point.

Monday, March 4th, three other guys and I flew into Long Binh to pick up some supplies for the platoon. As I indicated before, the PX at Lai Khe is very limited in merchandise, so we've been going to Long Binh to get what we need. There is an evacuation helicopter company in front of the hospital where they cleared away the trees. Whenever we go to Long Binh, we hitchhike on one of their helicopters... It was the first time I had ever flown in a helicopter. It is really interesting to see Vietnam from the air. We flew over Saigon and got a really good view of the Mekong River, which is actually wider than the Missouri in many places. After landing we went to the PX and returned to the helicop-

ter port where we had to wait until another ship returned to Lai Khe. One man got out that evening but three of us had to stay at the 93rd Evacuation Hospital, where I was initially assigned. Instead of sleeping under the stars, we went to the 93rd, which is on one side of the heliport, and asked them if they could lend us three blankets and litters. They did better than that; they told us to sleep in the baggage room. So, we got a good night's sleep. The next morning, we got a flight to Lai Khe about 11:00 a.m. It sure broke the boredom of sitting around waiting to depart. That night, before we went over to the 93rd, the other fellows, who were NCOs, and I went over to the NCO club. Since I was one stripe short of being an NCO, they rolled up my sleeves so my Specialist Four patches wouldn't show. We really had an enjoyable evening.

While we have been waiting to depart, we have been going to the movies regularly. The 18th Surgical shows a movie each evening. There is also a small medical unit across the road from us, which also shows movies each evening. I've seen two fairly good westerns in the last week. They were "The Way West" and "Rough Night in Jericho." Sometimes, when I watch a movie, I think how it was in San Antonio at the Majestic Theater, when I went to see movies there. There is little difference, you understand...

In many of his letters Buchta describes the important role the helicopters served in retrieving casualties from the field and bringing them quickly to field hospitals for treatment, substantially increasing the rate of survival. On other occasions, they hitched flights on the helicopters to go to larger military bases to pick up supplies.

I should be getting some black and white prints back in the next couple of days or so. Most of them were taken of men in the unit and some of the hospital. I'll send them home as soon as I receive them. I also got some good slides on my trip to Long Binh. I still have a few exposures left on the roll. It will be a while before the slides can be sent home. I sent two boxes of slides home. Tell me when you receive them.

I must close for this writing. Hope all of you are fine. Thanks for the boxes. Tell the dogs "hello" for me.

On March 6, 1968, while traveling as a passenger aboard an Air Force C-130 that was relocating his hospital unit from Lai Khe to Quang Tri, Buchta was invited to the flight deck by the navigator to take aerial photos of the Vietnamese countryside.

Roger

* * *

The deadly threats that abounded during the early days of Tet Offensive seemed to have all but disappeared, according to the tone shared in several of Buchta's letters. The medical duties at the hospital did not appear to be in any way overwhelming when compared to the experiences of other hospitals and clinics closer to some of the more heated areas of combat. Within days of his writing his previous letter, the 18th Surgical Hospital and 542nd Medical Company packed up their equipment on United States Air Force cargo planes on March 6, 1968, and flew to their new duty station at Quang Tri.[85]

---

[85] Buchta remarks that the airplane was a C-130 Hercules. As noted on the website of the Air Mobility Command Museum, "Beginning in 1965, the C-130

In his communications, Roger explained that their move required several of the large cargo planes. Each aircraft carried one of their 2-1/2-ton trucks with a trailer. One of the highlights of the trip, Buchta penned, was when the navigator on the C-130 he was a passenger aboard extended to him the opportunity to come to the flight deck and take some aerial photographs with his 35mm camera of the highlands and part of the coastal region. Within a short period of time, they would again begin to embrace a frenetic schedule of treating combat casualties. The last half of his tour of duty in Vietnam, Buchta discovered, would become the most intense and unyielding of his time served overseas and help pass the time quickly as he approached his awaited period of R&R and, finally, his return to the United States and discharge from the U.S. Army.

Hercules with its four turbo-prop engines, superior 15-ton payload and its ability to rapidly offload palletized cargo dominated airlift operations in Vietnam. Air Mobility Command Museum, *Airlift During the Vietnam War*, https://amc-museum.org.

CHAPTER 7

The Intensity of War

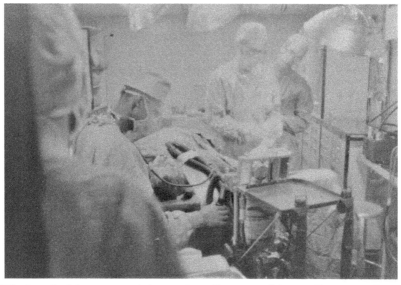

The hospital is now receiving quite a few casualties; in fact, it is almost at full capacity. They are having trouble evacuating the patients after surgery. Most of the patients are evacuated to a Navy ship a couple of miles off the coast. Some also are flown to larger hospitals in Da Nang. –Buchta explained in a letter written home on March 18, 1968.

B y March 11, 1968, Buchta and his fellow soldiers were essentially settled into their new surroundings at a military base a few miles south of the city of Quang Tri, making all the necessary preparations to get the hospitals up and running as quickly as possible to begin receiving the influx of casualties expected from the field. The northernmost province of South Vietnam near the DMZ, Quang Tri is located along the Thach Han River and, during the Vietnam War, evolved into "one of the most contested areas in South Vietnam where Hanoi troops constantly tried to infiltrate across the borders from Laos and North Vietnam."[86] As the Tet Offensive progressed, there were a number of battles that occurred in and around Quang Tri City, with the enemy engaged in intense fighting. Several of these battles lasted many weeks during and after Tet, since securing the area had the potential of opening an avenue of attack from the north. However, South Vietnamese forces, supplemented with U.S. Army and Marine troops, were able to hold their ground.

Immediately following their arrival at Quang Tri, the hospital personnel embarked upon a task that they had previously refined through much practice—setting up their living areas and the hospital. Initially, a small problem unfolded the first time it rained. After getting the tents erected in their assigned areas, they discovered that their new living spaces were within a dried-up rice paddy, and they had been in such a hurry to get everything set up that there had not been sufficient time to construct wood floors. These sloppy conditions resulted in a mad rush to beg, borrow, and steal any pieces of spare lumber that could be found—which was certainly a limited and sought-after commodity—to prevent the messy conditions from revisiting them the next time any adverse weather conditions decided to pay them a visit. An important supplement to their tents was the toilets and shower shed; however, with nearly one hundred

---

[86] Vietnam War Travel, *DMZ Quang Tri*, https://namwartravel.com.

men vying for the opportunity to shower and shave, many times these activities occurred in limited fashion by the water trailer until additional facilities could be established.

Another challenge facing the medical units was the lack of mess facilities, which would take some time to be erected and become operational. In the meantime, the Marines stationed in a nearby area of the base allowed the soldiers to use their mess area, which, strangely enough, Buchta explained, was situated in the middle of an old Vietnamese cemetery. Other times, when the mess facility was not available, the Marines at Quang Tri provided the medical soldiers with C-Rations. The "Type C Ration" was developed by the military prior to World War II and consisted of "individual, canned, pre-cooked meals [that] were issued to U.S. forces when fresh food and survival rations were unavailable and mess halls or field kitchens were inaccessible for the preparation of packaged, unprepared food."[87] Buchta described the canned meal as including a main dish with some type of meat, supplemented by a can of bread or crackers. The meal also included a spread and dessert such as fruit, dehydrated pudding, or fruitcake. He also mentioned the importance of the tinfoil packet accompanying the meal, which contained a spoon, cigarettes, instant coffee, salt, dried cream, salt, gum, etc. On occasion, many of the soldiers hoarded the C-Rations in case the food at the Marine mess hall was not to their individual tastes.

Work continued for the next several days with the men setting up the hospital so that it would be up and running. They worked in a smooth and efficient fashion. Roger's writings during this period

---

[87] Ohio History Connection, *What do you know about C-Rations?*, https://ohiohistory.org.

156

included some opining on the doctors, whom he described as occasionally using their positions as officers and physicians to care for their own comforts while the other personnel struggled to get everything ready to go as quickly as possible. The disarray and confusion from the move soon seemed to work itself out, and despite the aggravations that occurred, they got their respective areas up and running. The pace of activity certainly did not prevent the medical personnel from continuing their habit of imbibing in the spirits during their down time. This made for some interesting mornings, when large groups of soldiers strived to erect the large tents while concurrently having to nurse intense hangovers.

* * *

Shortly after arriving at Quang Tri, Buchta
(pictured) and several of his fellow soldiers were
sent to a sandy area near the base pick up sandbags
to be placed around the hospital. When getting
to the site, the soldiers paid Vietnamese locals a
penny for each sandbag loaded on their vehicles.

Sp/4. Roger Buchta
542nd Medical Company
Quang Tri, South Vietnam
March 14, 1968

Dear Mom, Dad and Don:

How's everything back home these windy March days? Anyway, it is supposed to be, I guess. Won't be long till it's time to get the hoe and garden seed out. Of course, there will be trot-lining, too.[88]

Well, the hospital is up. All four inflatables are up. Now we are just cleaning and preparing to receive our first patients. The living quarters are beginning to feel a bit more comfortable. While I am writing this, about fifteen guys from our unit, and a few from the 18th, are getting pretty high down at the other end of the tent. They have a couple of bottles of whiskey and a couple cases of beer…

As I started to say, the hospital is up and is supposed to begin receiving patients Friday, March 15th. The hospital won't be fully operational for about two more weeks. There is the problem of getting supplies. Many of the supplies are still at the airstrip, which is about a mile from our campsite. So, it will be a while before the hospital begins to function smoothly.

---

[88] A trotline is a length of fishing line with baited hooks at certain intervals that is stretched across an expanse of water.

We've been having some real good touch football games the last few evenings. The first evening we played, we chose sides with six men on each team. We really had fun. The Marines were playing in an area next to us. After the game, they came over and asked if we wanted to play them the next evening. They wanted to play tackle. That idea wasn't accepted too well. We declined their invitation on the grounds that tackle football was too dangerous. Some of us figured that they are Marines and, consequently, they wanted to do more than just play a friendly game of football. In a fair game, I think we could have beaten them. There are two men in the 542nd who played college football, one at South Dakota and the other at a small college in Minnesota. But we decided against playing them. Instead, we got a game with a team from the 18th Surgical. The game ended in a 12-12 tie. You can't believe how sore I was the next day when I got out of bed.

Enclosed in this letter is a money order for $130. My finance records are still screwed up. I still haven't received any E-4 pay. So, the Army owes me E-4 pay for three and a half months. They assured me I would receive the pay due to me this month or the next. The back pay should come to over $150.

I'll close for this time. Write when you can.

Roger

* * *

From Buchta's perspective, their arrival at Quang Tri unfolded during what seemed to be a period of relative calm. He also did not realize, however, was there was much activity occurring in the area. In the vicinity of nearby Khe Sanh, there had been a significant amount of enemy activity during the Tet Offensive. The action in the Khe Sanh area momentarily subsided in the early part of March 1968, around the timeframe Buchta arrived at nearby Quang Tri with the 542nd Medical Company. What he did not realize was that there were two divisions of the North Vietnamese Army preparing to close in on Khe Sanh. On March 17 [1968], only three days following Buchta's previous letter, it was noted that "the NVA/VC staged another assault and attempted to destroy a section of the outer perimeter. The following day, a full NVA battalion launched an attack on that sector. The combat was fierce, but after more than two hours, the Marines were able to repulse the assault."[89] Sporadic fighting would define the next few weeks and lead to casualties that would need to be treated while concurrently resulting in enemy threats in closer proximity to Quang Tri, which would have consequences for the 542nd Medical Company and their humane mission of trying to treat the wounded.

* * *

---

[89] Welsh, *The History of the Vietnam War*, 121.

Sp/4. Roger Buchta
542nd Medical Company
Quang Tri, South Vietnam
March 18, 1968

Dear Mom, Dad and Don:

I sure hope this letter finds you all well. I was sorry to hear, in your last letter, that grandma was sick recently. In the newspaper, which we receive daily, I noticed that the temps still haven't begun to warm up. But I presume they will warm up before long. Here, the weather has been very pleasant. I doubt if the mercury climbs above the 80-degree mark during the day. At night it gets downright cold, especially during the morning hours. During the day, we roll up the sides of the tent. For those who work at night, and sleep during the day, it is very comfortable.

The last few days we've been getting the hospital ready for its "grand opening." We were informed that the hospital would have to be completely sandbagged before patients could be received. So, that's primarily what's been occupying our time the past few days. There is not too much work involved the way we do it. The whole area is very sandy. One can dig down several feet in many places and never hit solid earth. The Vietnamese fill the bags, and we have to go and pick them up. Today four of us went to pick up a load of bags near the airstrip, which is about two miles from our camp. When we got there, we discovered that the Vietnamese would load them for a penny a bag. We chipped in and let them do the work. The filling is paid for by the government. While they loaded the bags, the four of us walked around the area and took pictures. The area where these people fill sandbags covers about five acres. On one side of the sand field is the airstrip; on the other side are gardens and a Buddhist nunnery. There must be at least 1,000 Vietnamese working at the sandbag area. You will see Vietnamese ranging in age from six to sixty working here. It is really funny to watch them fill the bags with their little shovels. It almost reminds me of children playing in the sand. The Vietnamese hardly ever sit down as we do, but they squat as if their bowels were moving. If you show them a chair, they will squat in it rather than sit in it. You can imagine how unusual they look at work. They also really enjoy themselves as they work. Occasionally the "Momma San," or lady in charge, will scold them if they play around too much. It's really funny.

Boys come around and try to sell you beer or soda. Beer costs a dollar a bottle and soda 70 cents. So, you see, they don't sell too much to us GIs. The boys do sell quite a bit to the Marines, who come in from the field. The Marines get rationed beer or none at all if it isn't available. When these Marines can get a beer, they are willing to pay exorbitant prices. The Vietnamese also sell liquor that is brewed in a government distillery. The smell of it alone can send you into orbit. The Marines, of course, will drink anything with alcohol in it...

The Marines frequently interacted with the hospital staff stationed Quang Tri. Buchta took this photograph of a group of Marines heading out on a mission in the spring of 1968.

Sunday night the hospital opened up for business. At first it was thought the opening would be delayed due to the lack of supplies. But a few days ago, the supplies started coming in. Now they have more than they know what to do with. The 18th Surgical has been receiving quite a few new men. As a result, we are able to work on eight-hour shifts. In our spare time we put flooring in our tents. Large pieces of plywood are used; so, we should be done quickly. As soon as the flooring is in, I want to make myself a desk and dresser. I'll have to go to the ammo dump across the road to get lumber for that.

*Artillery rounds come in long wooden boxes, which
are excellent for odds and ends calling for lumber.
The furniture may be crude, but it is functional.
After we are firmly established, spare time can be
devoted to recreation. One of our doctors brought a
volleyball and net from Qui Nhon recently.*

*So, that's about the way things stand at the
present time... Stay well and drop me a few lines
when you have the time.*

Roger

* * *

Several days later, Buchta remarks that the enemy activity occurring in nearby Khe Sanh has begun to settle down considerably. In
the third week of March, the hospital was up and running and had
begun to receive casualties, but not at the levels they had initially
anticipated given the circumstances in Khe Sanh. South Vietnamese
and U.S. forces believed that the North Vietnamese Army would
attempt to completely overrun Khe Sanh, but they failed in this
endeavor. Buchta's discussion with fellow soldiers, in addition to
reading military newspapers, left him with the understanding that
when the monsoons withdrew in the next few weeks, the NVA would
scramble from the area in fear of the overwhelming airpower that
U.S. could bring to bear. The monsoons the area was experiencing
during this time often left such an overcast that U.S. aircraft did not
have the visual clarity necessary to effectively levy an attack against
enemy forces.

Quang Tri, as Buchta described to his mother, was a large base on flat terrain. Again, seeking to ease his mother's concerns for his safety in a hostile overseas location, the soldier affirmed that he was much safer here than he had been at Lai Khe, because an attack could be seen from some distance, and the Marines stationed at the base were immediate to respond overwhelmingly to any threats emerging in the area. Additionally, he noted that similar to the conditions at Lai Khe, the hospital was situated in the middle of the sprawling camp and, therefore, unlikely to come under mortar or rocket attack. While patient concern was of utmost importance, he added, the military was not going to place a $7.5 million hospital in a dangerous area. The hospital area was also much quieter than it had been at Lai Khe, where it had been adjacent to the airstrip; at Quang Tri, they were approximately two miles from the airstrip and removed from much of the noise associated with landing or departure of aircraft.

The soldier also opined on the recent employment situation at Russellville High School, from which he had graduated nearly six years previous. His communications indicate that it was his belief that some good teachers had left the Russellville school system but that there was a glimmer of hope on the horizon since teacher salaries had undergone a mild increase, and the district was in the process of hiring additional staff to deliver education to the students. In 1968, the student body at Russellville had grown in enrollment to 322 high school students and 223 at the elementary level with more than twenty-three teachers hired to provide the instruction.[90] This was an important factor for Buchta, who had developed, in his mind, a plan to pursue his master's degree after receiving his discharge from the

---

[90] August 11, 1968 edition of the *Sunday News and Tribune*.

U.S. Army and find a high-school level teaching position in a district near his home in Lohman.

*   *   *

Sp/4. Roger Buchta
542nd Medical Company
Quang Tri, South Vietnam
March 26, 1968

Dear Mom, Dad and Don:

It's a cold, rainy-type evening here at Quang Tri. I was told that the monsoons were about over in this area, but apparently this wasn't true. The last few days have been heavily overcast, rainy, and cold. A few fellows even got out their field jackets; the same jackets that they laughed about when they were told they would have to take them to Vietnam. So, we're having a little back-home-type weather.

The past few days, I have been working in the hospital and troop area. The hospital is on twelve-hour shifts until it gets firmly established. The whole hospital, and all the tents, must be sandbagged. As a result, each section of the hospital has released some of its personnel to work on the outside. It's actually easier than working in the hospital. We work at the hospital about seven hours a day and then about two hours around our tent each day. It would seem to be hard work, but the way we do it, it isn't. The men work about thirty minutes and then take a thirty-minute break. The sandbags are filled and loaded on the trucks by the Vietnamese. All we have to do is unload the trucks and make the walls. In a few days, the hospital should be back on eight-hour shifts.

The hospital is now receiving quite a few casualties; in fact, it is almost at full capacity. They are having trouble evacuating the patients after surgery. Most of the patients are evacuated to a Navy ship, a couple of miles off the coast. Some also are flown to larger hospitals at Da Nang. A couple of days ago, they received a couple very unusual casualties. A trainer and his dog were hit by a mortar. Both of them got very superficial fragment wounds. While the trainer was being treated, I examined the dog. It was a bit funny to see that he had a field medical card just like the soldier who had been injured. He had some very small fragment wounds in his chest and right front leg. They were only skin deep. After the doctors examined him, they decided surgery wasn't necessary, because the pieces of lead would eventually work themselves through the skin. When the trainer came outside, he showed us some of the things the dog could do. His commands were barely recognizable to us but not to the dog. The trainer told us his dog is used primarily for mine and booby trap detection and for detecting an enemy ambush. He told us we would be surprised how many lives these dogs save. All of the dogs, of course, are German Shepherds. This particular canine was huge and utterly beautiful as far as color and markings are concerned. He was also very gentle. While I examined him, he continually kept his eye on the door anticipating the exit of his master.

While I am on the subject, I was wondering if Girl's leg is well-healed and if she limps? Send me a picture of her sometime. The hospital also received another dog and his trainer a few hours after I was off duty. I understand they had very minor wounds and, after treatment, were released. That's my dog story for this time.

This week I went on the laundry run to Quang Tri a couple of times. It's really ridiculous to take as little laundry as we have so far to a civilian laundry, but it's a chance to get away. It also gives us a chance to see what the city and area are like. Quang Tri must have a population of 250,000 or more. A huge river runs through the main part of the city. On one stretch of the river is a bridge that Charlie blew up.[91] The new bridge is heavily guarded by Vietnamese and MPs. There is quite a bit of French influence in the area. I noticed many Catholic churches and buildings of French origin...

---

[91] "Charlie" was slang used by U.S. troops during the Vietnam War to describe Viet Cong.

… My hand is getting a bit cramped, so that will have to be about all for now. Hope all of you are well and the snow doesn't return. I sure wish that you all have a warm Easter. Maybe the weather will be straightened out by then. Write soon.

Roger

* * *

Skirmishing in the Quang Tri Province was still a deadly reality, and, as Buchta noted, casualty counts were increasing at the hospital. As an individual who possessed a lifelong affinity for animals, specifically canines, it is of no surprise that he took great interest in treating and learning about the military working dogs that were brought to the hospital. The experience was certainly one that reminded him of his beloved dogs back in mid-Missouri and introduced him to many of the lifesaving tasks the ones in Vietnam had been trained to perform. German Shepherds, Buchta observed were the dogs of choice being used by the U.S. military. In the years prior to World War I, the German Army embraced selective breeding of German Shepherds to help develop in them "the traits of intelligence, loyalty, dedication, and tenacity needed for military and police applications… [and demonstrated] great promise in areas such as obedience, tracking, and protection."[92]

---

[92] Military Working Dog Team Support Association, *German Shepherd Dogs in the Military*, https://mwdtsa.org.

These promising canine soldiers would see use primarily with the German Army during World War I, but when the United States and other countries witnessed their capabilities, they began to train their own German Shepherds for military service. Military working dogs were used by the United States during World War II to perform such functions and provide an alert to prevent ambushes, and they also went on to perform with great distinction during the Korean War. In Vietnam, the United States embraced German Shepherds' initially as sentry dogs on Air Force installations, but, as the war progressed, they were utilized in a scout dog role. The military working dogs, with their heightened sense of smell and hearing, were critical to many infantry units. They located trip wires and mines while tracking down fleeing enemy units. These furry soldiers not only sniffed out bombs and other explosive devices that could harm U.S. and South Vietnamese soldiers. The canines could sniff out the tunnel systems used to conceal enemy forces who were often lying-in wait for the opportunity to emerge and launch surprise attacks.

Buchta's writings expose to an extent what developed into a life-long process of viewing his surroundings with an unbridled, childlike curiosity. Days earlier, he and his fellow soldiers had taken on the role of sightseers in a foreign land when visiting Buddhist structures at the nearby sand field, and, more recently, he wrote of his opportunity to depart the confines of the military base when on a laundry run for his company. But rather than being a chore, as it might have been for many, the trip impressed upon the medic some of the fascinating local structures and sites such as a bridge that had been replaced after being destroyed in an earlier battle in addition to seeing the Thach Han River for the first time. Even in the middle of war, where he often treated the wounds of both man and beast, Buchta never lost interest in learning more about the people, structures, and history of Vietnam. His reflections, in a sense, validate that he is by no means an Army careerist nor a military zealot. Rather Roger was a draftee who never shirked the responsibilities he has been given. In his letters home, he reveals that he has instead chosen a positive outlook regarding his circumstances and is making the best of whatever situation he may encounter in his military travels.

* * *

Sp/4. Roger Buchta
542nd Medical Company
Quang Tri, South Vietnam
March 31, 1968

Dear Mom, Dad and Don:

It's a fairly warm Sunday afternoon here in Quang Tri. The weather has been quite warm the past few days, although there has been a very comfortable breeze. Today I had off, but I have to go to work tonight. Tomorrow, I'll be off until Tuesday night. So, there will be a little free time in the next few days. This past week, everyone has been working like hell. Quite a few casualties have come in this week. Most of the injuries seemed to have resulted from booby traps or sheer carelessness. The other evening, for instance, a helicopter came in with seven wounded GIs and ARVNs (soldier of the Army of the Republic of Vietnam). It seems that the men were warming themselves around a fire when a hand grenade was accidentally shoved into the fire. It's really surprising sometimes to hear how many soldiers suffer non-combat injuries that just put them out of action.

Everyone has also been doing a lot of sandbagging and other odd jobs here and there. The hospital also set up some tents to be used as convalescent wards. This hospital is the only real medical facility in the area, except for a couple of ships off the coast. Many times, men with minor wounds that require medical attention over a short period of time have no choice but to stay at the 18th Surgical. Since the post-op inflatable wards are almost always full, some tents had to be pitched to care for men with minor wounds and illnesses. And, of course, the tents have to be sandbagged. We haven't had much time for recreation. The hospital is also on 12-hour shifts. I'll sure be glad when it goes back to eight-hour shifts. At night, however, they do show movies.

I have been doing a little work this week in my living area. I built a bookshelf and a desk. They are rather crude considering the materials at my disposal, but they are sturdy. If you want to make something out of lumber, it is necessary to use the materials at hand. I just started assembling bits of scrap lumber day after day. Finally, I decided to make what I could with the scraps...

I read in your last letter, dated March 22, that you purchased a jeep. You should really enjoy it. They're not only good for hunting, fishing, etc., but can be very handy around the farm. Most of the jeeps in Vietnam are made by Ford. They are fast enough to use on the road yet strong enough to do many jobs that a small tractor can do. What you should do is make you a trailer for it. All the jeeps in the Army come with trailers. You would be surprised how much they can carry. They aren't indestructible and will turn over easier than you think. I've seen several men who were hurt when they turned them over. Jeeps can be dangerous if you don't drive them carefully. Whatever you do, make sure it's not Army green when I come home. Ha! Incidentally, I have 188 days to go without an early separation. That still sounds like quite a few, doesn't it?

… That's about it for this time. All of you write if you get a chance.

Roger

* * *

A sad reality of the Vietnam War, Buchta explained to his family in an unvarnished manner, were the needless casualties that resulted from accidents such as the grenade that rolled into a fire next to a group of soldiers while also discussing the dangers posed by jeep rollover incidents. The process used to classify what constituted being reported as an accident during the war might not be abundantly clear; however, a report accessible through the National Archives Records Administration does provide some insight into the matter of casualty statistics. Information retrieved from the Vietnam Conflict Extract Data Files, created by the Defense Manpower Data Center of the Office of the Secretary of Defense, reveal that of 58,220 total casualty records, 9,107 of these incidents were categorized as accidents.[93] Many of the non-hostile deaths that would occur in Vietnam, and which Buchta does not mention but certainly would have witnessed, were those resulting from malaria—a mosquito-borne disease that, when left untreated, can develop into severe complications ending in death. A study appearing in *Clinical Infectious Diseases* explained that during the Vietnam War, "there were 24,606 cases of malaria, an estimated 391,965 sick-days because of malaria, and 46 deaths due to malaria."[94] This disease provided the various military hospitals with a unique medical challenge in addition to treating the combat wounded.

While Buchta was performing a variety of military duties at Quang Tri, there was, at the same time, a number of interesting developments with regard to the American support for the Vietnam War. The recent impact of the Tet Offensive had proven discouraging for President Lyndon Johnson, who came dangerously close to losing the Democratic nomination for the presidency to Senator Eugene McCarthy in the New Hampshire primary. Additionally, on March 31, 1968, a fateful moment in the war came when "Lyndon Johnson

[93] National Archives and Records Administration, *Vietnam Wars U.S. Military Fatal Casualty Statistics*, https://archives.gov.
[94] Beadle and Hoffman, *History of Malaria in the United States*, Abstract.

gave his televised speech to the nation restricting the bombing of North Vietnam and thereby renouncing any possibility of another term as president in order to hold the country together in the time he had left."[95] Days later, it would be announced that North Vietnam intended to return to negotiations with the United States, but these occurrences, in the highest level of government, would not immediately result in any noticeable changes in the daily schedules of Buchta and his fellow medical personnel.

---

[95] Sheehan, *A Bright Shining Lie*, 720-722.

CHAPTER 8

A Lingering War...

*"Everything has been fairly quiet in this area in the past day
as far as casualties that the hospital has received is concerned.
Actually, about two out of three casualties are ARVNs. The rest
being from 1st Cavalry Division. The Marines are generally
sent to hospital ships that are anchored off the coast." –*
Buchta explained in his letter home dated April 15, 1968

The first two weeks of April 1968 were quite soggy for the troops at Quang Tri. Though some might have expected mud to have been a cardinal challenge for the soldiers stationed there, Buchta explained that since the area was grassy with a high composite of sandy soil, the water that continued to fall from the sky appeared to drain well. The peace talks, which again began to burrow their way into the newsfeeds back home, became a part of the discussions that Buchta shared with his family in his letters. But, as he went on to opine, he and his fellow troops were inclined to dismiss such possibilities as little more than utter foolishness, believing the situation would linger on as before, and the medical staff would continue patching up the soldiers and Marines wounded in combat while also having the unenviable responsibility of preparing some of the less fortunate ones for body bags.

There was some promising news, Buchta maintained, that resulted from the favorable circumstances of recent successes of the U.S. Marines, 1st Cavalry Division and ARVN forces in repelling attempts of the Communist forces to seize Khe Sanh and some of the surrounding areas. Additionally, the U.S. and South Vietnamese forces were at the time embroiled in a major drive to secure the entire northern area of South Vietnam. When visiting with a lieutenant from the 1st Cavalry Division, Buchta was informed that their intelligence determined there were more than three divisions of the North Vietnamese Army operating in the northern region of South Vietnam, but that enemy movement had been significantly restricted because of heavy bombing and movement of the allied troops into the area. The tide had turned, Buchta was advised, and rather than trying to repel incursions into their strongholds, the Marines were now on the offensive while the 1st Cavalry Division occupied Khe

Sanh. He then learned that the 18th Surgical Hospital had been relocated to the base at Quang Tri to support this major operation.

The local news the soldiers received may have been understandably dominated by the activity in the northern sector of South Vietnam; however, certain events back in the states were also followed with abundant interest. One tragedy that Buchta viewed with great sadness was the death of Martin Luther King Jr., who was assassinated at a hotel in Memphis, Tennessee, on April 4, 1968. The news of the civil rights leader's death spread quickly throughout the world news outlets and, upon reaching Quang Tri, an African American soldier with whom Buchta was serving asserted that he was not going to work in the mess hall despite having been ordered to do so, since he was in mourning over the murder of King Jr. Demonstrating that the U.S. Army pauses for no tragedy and has unique methods in motivating compliance with issued orders, the grieving soldier was seen scrubbing pots and pans the next day.

The hospital operations had also slowed to the extent that the medical staff were able to return to eight-hours shifts. Assigned to the period of midnight to 8:00 a.m., Buchta remarked that few casualties were received during these hours, and that a good portion of his time was invested in replenishing supplies on the shelves, mopping the floors, and even catching a few winks of sleep on occasion. He and his fellow soldiers continued to enjoy games of volleyball, softball, and football on the rare occasions when there were enough soldiers available to participate. The medic also requested that his parents send him some batteries—the type of which was not available at their Post Exchange—for a small transistor radio that he had purchased from his platoon sergeant for the price of ten dollars. Prior to Buchta's acquisition of the radio, it had been won by his platoon sergeant during another off-duty activity several of his fellow soldiers embraced—games of poker.

* * *

Sp/4. Roger Buchta
542nd Medical Company
Quang Tri, South Vietnam
March 31, 1968

Dear Mom, Dad and Don:

It's Easter here in Quang Tri. Surprisingly, it has seemed like Easter—just in a different way. It worked out that I was off today, so I guess I was fortunate in that respect. This morning some of us went to church. Services are held in a tent. Every seat was taken. There were many fellows here from different units in the area. There were even some Marines present. The minister really had a fine sermon. This afternoon, I got a little shuteye and did a little reading...

Everything has been fairly quiet in this area for the past few days as far as casualties that the hospital has received is concerned. Actually, about two out of three casualties received are ARVNs. The rest are from the 1st Cavalry Division. The Marines are generally sent to the hospital ships that are anchored off the coast. There are two ships used for hospitals; when one is full, they sail to Okinawa or Da Nang and unload their patients. Of course, the ship is capable of receiving and treating many casualties before it has to unload its patients. When there is a mass casualty situation, the ships receive ARVN as well as American troops. There is an ARVN hospital in Quang Tri, which is staffed by three Navy doctors and two Vietnamese doctors; so, you can see that this hospital is limited in the number of casualties it can receive. The Vietnamese army has been very active in this area of Vietnam. It seems they are assuming more and more of the burden of this war. The American press has criticized the Vietnamese army continuously for being cowardly and unwilling to take an active role in the war. In the last few months, there have been very few incidences where ARVN units have retreated or not towed their share of the load. The American press fails to recognize the fact that, until a few years ago, South Vietnam didn't have an army or equipment to supply one. If the Vietnamese army hasn't been as active as many people feel it should have been, it was Westmoreland's fault. Now, there is greater stress on enabling the ARVNs to carry a heavier load in the war. They are being armed with M-16 rifles and other modern weapons. When the allied forces halt operations, policing up will have to rest with the Vietnamese army. The allies are finally recognizing this.

The 1st Cavalry Division and Marines are really raising hell in Quang Tri Province... The 1st Cavalry, or a couple of units of it, are occupying Khe Sanh while the Marines and other 1st Cavalry units are making a giant sweep of the area. Enemy contact is becoming less and less frequent, meaning simply that the enemy has fled, probably back across the border. The ARVNs are sweeping the south to prevent the NVA from escaping to the south. The whole situation seems to be very promising. We get news about the operations first-hand since the hospital receives casualties from these operations. I always like to chat with the men while they are waiting to go to surgery. Mom, you mentioned that you heard the enemy, fleeing from Khe Sanh, were heading for Quang Tri. Apparently, you misinterpreted what you heard. If the enemy fled toward Quang Tri, it would be sheer suicide for them. Their only route of escape is to the north or west, where the jungle could provide them with cover. The terrain around Quang Tri city, and the base here is very flat and lacks cover. Perhaps, if operations are successful in this area of Vietnam, the NVA will be more willing to come to the peace table.

So much for the situation over here. What happened to Girl? In the picture you sent, Girl looked like a big round pillow. She is what I call knocked up. Glad to hear she is doing well. Take good care of her. How are Sissy's eyes? I have been wondering

*if she is completely blind by now. I sure hope she
retains at least partial vision.*

*That's about all the gossip I can think of for
this time. Hope you all had a very happy Easter…
So long and write when you can.*

Roger

* * *

The 18th Surgical Hospital was a single component of a large
structure of medical support facilities operating in support of the
Vietnam War. Buchta alluded to many other medical support facilities such as the U.S. Navy hospital in Da Nang. He also referenced
the two ships moored off the coast of Vietnam—the USS *Sanctuary*
and the USS *Repose*. Both of these vessels were floating hospitals
launched during World War II and, during their service in Vietnam,
each became "a fully equipped hospital with 30 nurses and about 700
beds." These hospital ships could often be reached within minutes by
helicopter, and, because of their location off the coast of Vietnam,
they were credited with achieving a high recovery rate among the
Marines they treated. As a testament to dedication of those who
served aboard these medical ships during the war, "the 90 or more
Navy nurses serving at the Da Nang hospital and on the two hospital ships… are all volunteers." Despite the long hours worked while
engaged in the various medical responsibilities, one nurse explained
that the reward for serving in locations where they lacked many of

the comforts of home was the look of gratitude they received when treating the wounded.[96]

Mention is also made of "Westmoreland" in Buchta's previous letter. General William C. Westmoreland "commanded the United States forces in Vietnam from 1964-1968, overseeing the vast troop buildup and the height of the fighting..."[97] He was a graduate of the U.S. Military Academy at West Point and commanded an artillery battalion during World War II. In the years after Vietnam, Westmoreland was subject to great criticism due to his handling of the war. However, he would later maintain that the poor performance of the South Vietnamese Army, in addition to poor tactical decisions made by President Lyndon Johnson, were the primary reasons the war effort deteriorated. The ninety-one-year-old general passed away, in his native South Carolina, on July 18, 2005 and was laid to rest in the cemetery of his beloved West Point.

Buchta also noted that, during the early part of April, he had encountered a soldier from mid-Missouri who had grown up in the nearby community of Linn. They were able to share some stories about old high school rivalries and basketball games before parting ways for their separate duty assignments. It was also during this timeframe, the medic explained, that an Australian officer brought to their hospital a fourteen-year-old girl who was nearly blind from complications related to typhoid fever. Sadly, the hospital did not have the capabilities to treat such an illness, and the girl was transported to a Navy hospital ship where they had specialists who might be able to address her medical complications. Buchta later learned

---

[96] August 1, 1968 edition of the *Daily Journal*.
[97] July 19, 2005 edition of the *New York Times*.

that the young girl, who had come from a refugee center in Quang Tri, did not regain her eyesight. Her illness had been allowed to progress far too long.

There were other horrific and deadly circumstances that evolved in absence of enemy involvement, details of which were often kept out of the newsfeeds back in the states. On or about April 10, 1968, the 588th Signal Company of the U.S. Army hosted a live band inside their service club at Quang Tri. Buchta went on to detail that a group of Marines wanted to join the festivities but were told they would have to watch from outside because the club was overflowing with spectators. Angry from being denied entry, one of the Marines lobbed a tear gas grenade into the middle of the club while, in the confusion, another Marine cast a live hand grenade in the midst of the audience. One soldier was killed, another critically injured, and five others had fragmentation wounds. The Marines were scheduled to depart the next morning for various combat missions; however, the Provost Marshall issued a directive that all Marine elements would not be allowed to leave the base until the responsible parties were apprehended. The following day, Buchta learned through the grapevine, those responsible for the deadly incident were apprehended.

A couple of days following the grenade episode, excitement again electrified the hospital staff when a soldier came in seeking treatment for his pet ocelot—a medium-sized wildcat—that he had purchased when visiting Saigon. The animal was paralyzed from its hips back to its rear, and an x-ray performed by hospital staff revealed it had an intestinal obstruction. The veterinarian assigned to the surgical hospital utilized the hospital's operating room, but the ocelot did not survive the surgical procedure.

* * *

Sp/4. Roger Buchta
542nd Medical Company
Quang Tri, South Vietnam
April 19, 1968

Dear Mom, Dad and Don:

How's everything back home these nice warm spring days? I know it's been fairly warm back home, because I read in the Army newspaper what the temps are in Kansas City and St. Louis... In this part of the world the weather has been very nice. Days are sunny, but there's almost always a very gentle breeze. It does get quite hot around noon, however. A couple of days ago, one of the huge generators that supplies... the operating rooms with air-conditioning and electricity broke down. It became so unbearably hot we had to wait outside. Two casualties were awaiting surgery but had to wait until the generator was repaired and the operating room cooled off. You can imagine how hot the inflatable units would be without air-conditioning. At night, however, it is very pleasant.

On the evening of April 19, 1968, Buchta exited the mess hall at Quang Tri and received the unexpected surprise of a Marine Corps band touring the area and playing selections of popular music.

Things have really quieted down in this part of Vietnam. Operation Pegasus, comprising elements of the 1st Cavalry and Marines was designed to pacify the area around Khe Sanh. It was supposed to be one of the major operations of the war. As soon as the 1st Cavalry started sweeping around Khe Sanh and east to the Laotian border, the NVA pulled out. The major objective of the drive has been met, namely to pacify the whole area south of the DMZ. We are receiving very few casualties as the result of hostile action… The Marines are beginning to come back to their base camp, where the 18th Surgical is presently situated. They're recouping for another operation. The rumor is that another operation is being planned near Hue, in a place called A Shau Valley, which has long been a communist sanctuary. The Marines, ARVNs, and

1st Cav will conduct the operation. Until now, the Marines have primarily held, supposedly, strategic points such as Con Thien and Khe Sanh. It now seems they are going on the offensive.[98] When the operation begins, we'll be getting casualties again.

Today, when I went to dinner, I stepped out the door and saw a huge band behind the mess hall, instruments and all. There must have been at least thirty men in this group. It seems that a Marine band was touring the camp. They stopped at the various units and put on a brief performance. They played several popular selections such as "I Left My Heart in San Francisco" and "Shadow of Your Smile," etc. It was undoubtedly the best amateur band I've ever heard. It was very enjoyable dinner music. The Army really looks out for the comfort of its men. You can't beat live dinner music in a combat zone.

Another fellow and I are planning our R&R at this stage in our tour. He and I have about the same interests regarding what we want to see. He was going to go a week before me so we decided to go together, if it works out… I decided on going to Taipei and he did the same after investigating various factors about this R&R area. Taipei has the largest museum of Oriental culture in the world. It's called the National

---

[98] Also known as Cồn Tiên, Con Thien was situated near the Demilitarized Zone and although initially serving as a U.S. Army Special Forces camp, later transitioned to a combat base for the United States Marine Corps.

Palace Museum. Formosa probably provides the best sampling of Oriental culture in any country in the Orient. This R&R center is one of the more expensive centers but I think it will be worth it...

That's about the extent of the news for this time. Isn't April really flying by?... Five months and a few days is about all I have left between now and the time I board that beautiful Braniff bird and head east.[99] A few of us who leave 'Nam about the same time figured out the other night that our replacements are in their third week of basic. One fellow said he heard his replacement doing ten pushups for dropping his rifle... Another said he was so short he tripped over a razor blade. Everybody dreams they are shorter than they actually are. Then, when they actually get short, they flip out. It's really hilarious to watch the different reactions sometimes.

I hope the fish are biting, the garden is growing, and everyone's chipper. Dad, keep baiting those hooks, but save a few for me. Give my regards to everyone, and jot down a few lines when you can.

Roger

* * *

---

[99] Braniff International Airways was one of the companies chartered to operate the "Freedom Birds"—the aircraft that brought the troops home from the Vietnam War.

The operations in and near Khe Sanh continue to be a focal point of many of Buchta's letters, because he realizes his mother is reading about some of these missions in the newspapers back home and knows that her son is engaged in the medical treatment of many of the men belonging to the units involved. *Operation Pegasus*, which he briefly describes as an operation that did not meet with the anticipated resistance or result in a great number of casualties for the 18th Surgical Hospital, was reported to be much more intense combat by some news sources of the period, and resulted in a high casualty count for the North Vietnamese Army. Within a week of fighting in early April 1968, a reported 640 Communists had been killed. As of April 7, it was reported that "U.S. losses in *Operation Pegasus* were placed at 59 killed and 427 wounded. This included 31 Army men killed and 28 Marines killed, and 162 Army men wounded and 265 Marines wounded."[100] Brigadier General Oscar Davis, of the 1st Cavalry Division, forecasted doom for any of the Communist forces seeking to escape the region under the deadly sweeps of U.S. and South Vietnamese forces. A defining moment of the operation included the success of allied forces in the recapture of Lang Vei—a "demolished U.S. special forces camp near Laos…" The recapture of the base was of "symbolic as well as strategic importance" since its initial loss had been demoralizing for the allied forces It also signified the forfeiture of a valuable point from which to observe movement in the area.[101]

Sometime during this period, there had been several soldiers killed in action who were brought into the hospital to have their

---

[100] April 9, 1968 edition of the *Arizona Republic*
[101] April 13, 1968 edition of *The Spokesman-Review*.

remains prepared for transport back to his respective home. As Buchta would recount, to his older brother many years later, but chose not to mention in his letters home was one soldier that he recalled being very muscular and tall. The soldier's frame made it very difficult for the slender medic to wrestle his remains into a body bag. The man happened to be an Australian soldier, and, upon initial glance, there was no evidence of wounds incurred; however, closer examination revealed that, although he had been wearing his flak jacket, it had not been tied shut. This oversight allowed enough of an opening for a piece of shrapnel from a rocket to penetrate the soldier's chest and pierce his heart.

Again, Buchta turns an eye to the promise of R&R, demonstrating his zeal for learning when selecting a site to enjoy his time off, which he feels will offer the greatest opportunity to indulge in experiencing Asian history and culture. R&R was viewed by many service members as a time to relax on a beach, while sipping various types of fruity cocktails, and perhaps engaging in activities of questionable morality; yet for Buchta, he was well on his way to becoming a student of life, and such frivolities did not appear to be of interest to him. It also becomes evident, through his remarks, that Roger was well versed in world history, referring to Taiwan as Formosa—a historical reference to the Japanese-controlled island that was seldom used by anyone not familiar with its troubled past. Additionally, sections of his letters assume a lighter air, continuing to reveal his sense of humor and enjoyment of trading lighthearted and mirthful conversations with friends, who were growing closer to their time to return home.

It would be more than a month before Roger's next letter arrived home. Many events would pass, but one of the most heart wrenching came on April 30, 1968, when he dealt with a casualty whose brother, unexpectedly, he would meet decades later due to an informal conversation.

A Casualty Connection

Staff Sergeant Charles Lee Frisby was killed in action in the Quang Tri Province of South Vietnam on April 30, 1968. *Courtesy of Dana Frisby*

The latter weeks of April 1968 brought a welcome lull in activity for Buchta and the staff of the 18th Surgical Hospital. Three months earlier had heralded the beginning of the Tet Offensive. The results were many casualties that needed to be treated. This was followed by *Operation Pegasus*, which became one of the largest offensive operations of the war by South Vietnamese and U.S. forces. This period of calm for the medical personnel at Quang Tri soon

came to an end, leaving Buchta with powerful memories that would be resurrected decades later when he unexpectedly met one of the family members of a casualty he placed in a body bag.

"My older brother, Charles Lee Frisby, was born in 1944 with most of his right ear missing," said Russellville resident Dana Frisby. "There was another infant in the East St. Louis area born with an identical issue, so a doctor removed part of my father's lower rib and used the bone and grafted skin to construct an ear for both my brother and the other child." He added, "Years later, my brother was married and living in East St. Louis when he decided to join the U.S. Army in 1966. His ear never looked completely natural, and we thought he might have hearing loss, which might prevent him from being eligible for the military, but he was able to enlist."

Deploying to Vietnam in early 1968 during the large-scale, coordinated attacks by North Vietnamese forces that became known as the Tet Offensive, Frisby was assigned to 3rd Squadron of the 5th U.S. Cavalry. Given little time to adjust to his new surroundings, Frisby was quickly immersed in combat operations and leading troops in the vicinity of Quang Tri near the DMZ, which at the time continued to swarm with enemy activity.

While leading his platoon on patrol on April 30, 1968, Frisby and his fellow soldiers were attacked by an overwhelming force of North Vietnamese troops. During the firefight that ensued, Frisby and every soldier in his platoon were killed. Fortunately, their bodies were recovered and transported to the military base at Quang Tri.

Buchta happened to be one of the medical personnel on duty at the hospital at the time and was responsible for processing the remains of the casualties, collecting their information, and placing them in body bags. Frisby's body, thought disfigured from the battle, left imprinted memories with Buchta that would be awakened decades later.

"My brother's body was eventually brought home, and he was buried in Jefferson Barracks National Cemetery in St. Louis," said Dana Frisby. "My mother was quite distraught over losing her son, and I don't believe that she ever fully recovered from it." He continued, "At the time of his death, I was fifteen years old, and my brother's wife was still living in East St. Louis. One of the saddest parts of it all was that when he was killed, he had two daughters... both under three years old."

The pain of loss has not diminished by the passage of years, demonstrated by Dana's mournful explanation that when his brother's remains were returned home, the only recognizable part of his upper body was his right ear.

In later years, Dana moved to the community of Russellville, Missouri, only a few miles from where Buchta resided, and became the co-owner of Vault Pizza & Sandwiches. One day in 2014, while working at the restaurant, Dana and a regular customer of the establishment, Don Buchta, discussed the service of their brothers in the Vietnam War.

"Don said that his brother, Roger Buchta, was in Vietnam the same time that my brother was killed," said Dana Frisby. "He said that he should bring his brother up to visit with me about it, and I told him that would be fine, but I didn't think much more about it."

Several days later, Don brought Roger into the restaurant to speak with Dana, and the three engaged in what became a very lengthy, emotional conversation.

"When I described to Roger what happened to my brother's platoon, he said that he was at Quang Tri at that time and helped put the bodies of my brother's platoon in body bags while processing their remains," said Dana. Following an emotional pause, he added, "He remembered my brothers disfigured right ear and his unique last name."

The younger Frisby admits he was at first skeptical, but the detail of Buchta's reflections regarding specific circumstances of that fateful day convinced him of the validity of the correlation. Additionally,

Buchta's miltary records reveal that he was in fact working at the hospital at Quang Tri during this timeframe.

For years, Buchta quietly carried the weight of his time in the Vietnam War, seldom sharing with anyone other than his brother and close friends the experiences of witnessing egregious wounds of men his own age. Connecting with a family member, decades after processing the remains of their loved one, became yet another story Roger did not freely discuss. Sadly, Buchta has since passed, joining in eternal rest the scores of young soldiers he witnessed perish during the tense days of the Vietnam War.

"East St. Louis and Russellville may only be a couple hours or so apart, but what are the chances of meeting the guy who put your brother in a body bag in a war 10,000 miles away from home several decades earlier," Dana Frisby remarked. "Both Roger and my brother are no longer here, but that conversation did provide our family with some closure," he continued. "I appreciate what Roger did, and I know it wasn't easy for him to share that information, but I find solace knowing that he was professional in his duties, and my brother's remains were treated in a respectable manner."

CHAPTER 9

Closer to Home

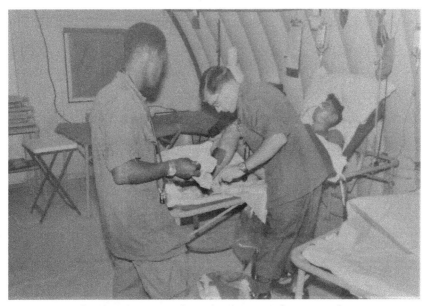

"A couple of nights ago, about 10:00 at night, a couple Marines brought in a woman, her mother, and a small child only six months old who was suffering from pneumonia and was just about dead. The woman and her mother were crying. The woman was certain her baby was going to die." –Buchta describing an event that unfolded at the hospital in Quang Tri in the second week of June 1968.

The pen of Roger Buchta gave the impression that it must have run out of ink for most of the month of May 1968. When he did finally communicate with his family, on the twenty-fourth of the month, his remarks were focused on an activity he greatly enjoyed back in Missouri—fishing. He noted that the letter he recently received from his father indicated the creeks back home were flowing at levels much lower than normal and if conditions were not to improve by the time he returned home later in the year, all of the fishing he wished to accomplish would only be possible in the ponds on the farm or the Missouri River a few miles north of their property.

The casualties received at the hospital had finally settled down to a level between light and moderate, since no major pushes had recently been conducted in the area. It was during this time, however, that Roger's intuition helped him save a friendly soldier who might otherwise have been left for dead.

Don Buchta recalled, "Roger told me several times about this South Vietnamese general who had been seriously wounded in combat near Quang Tri and was brought to their hospital for treatment. The general was unresponsive, and he was told to prepare him for a body bag because it was assumed that he was dead, but Roger had a feeling that he could be revived. Roger began giving the general repeated chest compressions, and he soon began breathing on his own and survived."

The section of the hospital in which Roger worked was, at the moment, busy with such mundane tasks as conducting sick calls in the mornings with an M.D. and medical practitioner who were on duty to address any medical problems of the soldiers reporting for treatment. Yet it did not mean that the doctors, or the medics assisting with sick call, were in any way resting on their laurels, since an average of between forty to fifty soldiers showed up seeking medical care. The problems the medical staff often addressed ranged from such issues as diarrhea to malaria and hepatitis. Additionally, the medics were administering shots that included the plague vaccine, which was used 'to immunize US troops during the Vietnam War, because plague was fairly common in Vietnam at the time."[102] Other shots being provided were the result of what Buchta described as "loose sexual practices," and included the antibiotic penicillin, which helped treat some of the sexually transmitted diseases contracted by the troops during their off-duty escapades.

Sick call, despite the number of soldiers seen and treated on a daily basis, was a manageable event, since everyone had specific duties to perform and they did so without hesitation or complaint. Occasionally, sick call could become rather hectic when a group of casualties were received from the field and triage re-prioritized their duties. Routinely, many of the tasks Buchta performed, in addition to giving shots to patients, was to take vital signs for the doctors and document the results in the patient's medical records. Other times, when the hospital became overwhelmed, because of combat casualties, he would process the remains of those killed in action, placing them in body bags so their remains could be shipped back to the United States for burial.

Don Buchta, the medic's older brother, remarked, "When Roger worked with placing soldiers in body bags, this was a very difficult task for him to perform. He never forgot that most of the men

---

[102] University of Minnesota, *US, UK, Canada to jointly test plague vaccines*, https:// cidrap.umn.edu.

were his age, and it was just one of those disheartening images that remained with him for the rest of his days."

* * *

Sp/4. Roger Buchta
542nd Medical Company
Quang Tri, South Vietnam
June 3, 1968

Dear Mom, Dad and Don:

It's a rainy and very gloomy day in this part of Vietnam. It's Monday but it seems like those gloomy, rainy Sunday afternoons that I remember back home. Today is my day off. The tent is very quiet for a change. One fellow is recording a letter to his girl; another is taking a nap; and I, of course, am writing a letter. The weather has been very unusual the past few days. The rain really ranges from light to heavy. A couple days ago there was a real downpour. As I said before, our camp is situated in old rice paddies. They have been filled in with sand on one side of the camp. The living area is on real low ground. When it rained you can imagine what happened, there was more than a foot of water in some tents including mine. My area, however, was on high ground, so I had no problem. Some guys came back from work and found boots and other things that were on the floor under water. In some areas between the tents, the water was two feet deep. A lot of guys stripped down to their shorts and went swimming; some were even floating around the tents on air mattresses. It was all unbelievable…

Business at the hospital has been very slack the past week or two. In fact, we've received so few casualties that they were able to close down two wards and put the ward personnel on eight-hour shifts. The ward people were really thrilled about this…

A few minutes ago, Dwight Verbeck, with whom I am going on R&R, and I walked over to the Marine PX. We heard the PX had gotten in some suitcases and thought we would check them out. He bought a large suitcase for $32.50. The suitcases were larger than I wanted, so I believe I'll wait. I do want to buy a couple of suitcases before leaving Vietnam because of all the junk I have to take home and the fact that I'm going to Europe next summer if I can save enough money. In about twenty days we'll be leaving on R&R. When I return, I'll have less than 100 days to go. I'll leave Vietnam October 5th, or shortly before that date…

Hope everyone is doing well and the fish start biting soon. Give everyone my best and write soon.

Roger

* * *

The hospital maintained a slow arc of activity, averaging approximately ten surgical patients on a daily basis, according to Buchta. His reflections, during this period, include several memories of hospital staff treating soldiers and civilians from the local area for a variety of diseases and maladies including hepatitis, malaria, sunstroke, leukemia, tetanus, heart attacks, and bubonic plague. On other occasions, the medical staff were unsuccessful in diagnosing the specific issues being suffered by soldiers and civilians alike and often had to focus on treating the symptoms. An additional, serious medical situation they dealt with were cases of rabies that were the result of canine and rat bites. Snake bite cases also became a recurring issue along with scorpion stings. Buchta noted that, in the instance of scorpion and centipede stings, the doctor would generally only provide treatment if the site of the sting became infected. When treated, the doctor applied an icepack and gave an injection of Benadryl. Buchta shared that he had recently been stung in chest by some sort of flying insect and a couple of days later, the site of the sting turned a pale, whitish color and started to drain. He then began applying antibiotic ointment and the infection disappeared within a few days, although a small scar remained as a reminder of his encounter with the unidentified insect.

* * *

Sp/4. Roger Buchta
542nd Medical Company
Quang Tri, South Vietnam
June 16, 1968

Dear Mom, Dad and Don:

Before I began this letter, another fellow and I were having a contest to see which one of us could kill the most fleas. I think he beat me, but I didn't lose by far. My whole area is littered with fleas. Ha! What we do for entertainment sometimes.

The month of June is already half over. Where does time go? How's everything back home? I bet the crops are really growing, since you all have received some rain. Over here, the weather is hot and dry. Occasionally, we receive a good shower, but the effects of it are short-lived. When that vicious sun starts beating down after the shower, everything is soon dry and dusty again. Well, that's Vietnam, I guess.

In about a week, another fellow and I will be leaving for Taipei. Our R&R begins June 25th and ends July 1st. Of course, we'll be able to kill about two weeks before we return. We'll leave the 18th Surgical Hospital the 23rd. If I'm not wrong, the two of us will leave from Da Nang by commercial jet. When we get back, we'll both be under a hundred days [remaining in Vietnam].

One of the activities that Buchta noted he enjoyed were the occasions they took their military trucks to the Quang Tri River to wash while at the same time enjoying a respite from the heat by donning their shorts and going for a swim.

Everything at the hospital has been slow as usual. This week the X-Ray machine broke down. The hospital had to close down for about three days. Only medical patients were admitted. A couple of nights ago, about 10:00 at night, a couple of Marines brought in a woman, her mother, and a small child only six months old who was suffering from pneumonia and was just about dead. The woman and her mother were crying. The woman was certain the baby was going to die. The doctor prescribed a mixture of IV (intravenous) fluids and drugs, which we immediately mixed up. Unable to find a vein in the child's arm or legs, through which the fluids and drugs could be administered, the doctor had to give the fluids through a vein on the side of the baby's head. It was all most interesting. Three days later, the baby was crying and well. They transferred her to the civilian hospital in Quang Tri, where I'm sure she's doing fine... Most Vietnamese, civilians and ARVNs are transferred to the ARVN or civilian hospitals in Quang Tri when they come to us from the field.

The hospitals in Quang Tri are severely limited in the services they can perform. As a result, if the doctors know that these services cannot be performed in Quang Tri, they perform surgery at this hospital and then transfer these patients to the hospital in Quang Tri. Many times, it is left to the discretion of the doctor whether he wants to treat a Vietnamese, especially civilians, with severe illnesses. The medical doctor here at the 18th Surgical is very good about treating civilians, especially children, who he knows may die if they are treated at a civilian hospital. When a Vietnamese is a patient here, there is almost always someone who stays with the patient, whether it be relatives or friends. These people have to sweep floors and empty trash just like any other patient who's able. The other day, they had this child's mother and grandmother, that I mentioned earlier, sweeping and working as though they were part of the ward crew. I don't think any of the patients minded because the woman was young and quite good looking.

I received the tapes you sent me last week. They were very clear and well-chosen selections, although the songs by Jim Reeves and John Gary made me a bit homesick... I'll close for this time. Hope all of you are well. Write soon.

Roger

* * *

As a spectator to life, Buchta would often relate to his family some of the non-military, cultural aspects of his surroundings that he witnessed. It was fascinating for him to discover how few Buddhist temples existed in the area; instead, Catholicism appeared to be the overarching religion of choice based upon the number of Catholic monasteries and churches he stumbled upon during his travels in and around Quang Tri. Near the central section of the military base at Quang Tri, which was being used by the Marine Corps, there stood a Catholic monastery that was encircled by barbed wire. There were signs posted about the place that denoted it as off limits to U.S. personnel. Seeking to quell some of his insatiable curiosity regarding local religious practices, Buchta and a fellow soldier crawled through an open section of the wire surrounding the site and quietly looked around the area. They marveled at the architecture of the monastery and the picturesque and decorative tombs in the adjacent cemetery. When leaving the grounds, the two caught sight of two monks who had been watching them from their perch in an upper floor of the abbey, thus inspiring their departure from the grounds of the holy site at a swift pace.

On one section of the military base at Quang Tri was a Catholic monastery surrounded by a fence with signs telling U.S. troops to stay off the property. Buchta and another soldier snuck though an opening of the fence, where he took this picture of the cemetery area near the monastery.

When visiting the marketplace in the city of Quang Tri, Buchta developed a severe dislike for those profiting from the black market. He would later maintain that many of these markets sold U.S.-manufactured items needed by the soldiers that were not available through their normal supply networks or at the Post Exchange. In frustration, he explained that the hospital had been in dire need of a suction machine for the past three months but were not able to acquire one through U.S. Army supply channels; however, it was later discovered that a Vietnamese vendor possessed a stolen suction machine that was spotted for sale at a roadside market. Although it was his greatest wish to see the authorities "throw the book" at those profiting through robbing the government, he admitted that he rarely heard of anyone being prosecuted for such thefts. In fact, he spoke with great irritation about a soldier in his own company who had stolen items from the hospital to trade for candy, cigarettes, and other comfort items, but who had yet to be caught in the act. There were times, Buchta explained, when wounded Viet Cong troops had been found wearing articles of clothing that had been stolen from the U.S. government. This entire scenario, the former medic asserted, resulted in a handful of "crooks" who were making a small personal fortune at the expense of the U.S. taxpayers.

Dissatisfaction with perceived thefts of government property would by no means sour the elation Roger felt with regard to his approaching vacation—or R&R—to the capital city of Taiwan. The island of Taiwan had once been under control of the Japanese government, but after World War II, control was transferred to the Republic of China. One of the locations Roger most looked forward to visiting during his respite, the National Palace Museum, housed an unbelievably vast collection of relics and artifacts from ancient Chinese history. For a studious individual who had spent years reading and absorbing countless morsels of world history, such an opportunity represented one of those unique moments when all that was learned through various history texts soon came to life before his eyes.

* * *

Sp/4. Roger Buchta
542nd Medical Company
Quang Tri, South Vietnam
June 22, 1968

Dear Mom, Dad and Don:

I hope this letter finds you all well and in a cool place on these hot summer days. Everything around the 18th Surgical seems to be moving along as usual. The weather is hot and balmy...

Tomorrow, Dwight Verbeck and I will be leaving for R&R.[103] *We will go to the R&R processing at Da Nang and wait there until our plane leaves for Taipei Tuesday afternoon. As I mentioned before, we will fly to Taipei by commercial jet. We will get back about July 2nd. Another fellow from our unit will be going to Da Nang with us. He is going to Hong Kong. I talked to a man who was stationed in Formosa [Taiwan] for a while. He spoke very highly of the people, shopping opportunities, food, and tourist attractions. He assured me that I would really enjoy my vacation there, so I hope he's right.*

This evening we are supposed to have a volley-ball tournament with the Marines. A few days ago, some Navy engineers leveled a patch of land for us,

---

[103] A native of Colorado, the fifty-seven-year-old Dwight L. Verbeck passed away on December 26, 2004, and was interred in Fort Logan National Cemetery in Denver, Colorado.

so we could put up a net. Actually, I haven't gotten to play yet for one reason or another. I did put my name on a list to play in the tournament. I bet I'll be so clumsy and uncoordinated from lying around that I'll fall about fifty times. Almost everyone participates in the games if they aren't working. We also put up a basketball goal quite a while ago. But I'm getting too old for the rigors of basketball. Ha!

Business at the hospital has been about the same as usual, although we seem to be getting a few more surgical patients the last few days. Most of these are fragment wounds. Last night, we got a man in who was on perimeter guard near Hue when an enemy rocket landed nearby. When they brought him in, he looked like a strainer. He had a severe chest wound, four limb fractures, and numerous flesh wounds. When he was on the chopper, his heart stopped beating. They revived him and kept him alive until we could start giving him blood and performing other lifesaving measures. He was in surgery for six hours. I hear that he seems to be alright, and the chances are good that he will make it. A few days ago, they also brought a woman in who had a bad chest wound. A day after she came out of surgery, she began to have labor pains. A nurse and medic delivered the baby, which was two months premature. Of course, it was dead. The birth was completely unexpected. The woman is getting along well. That sure must have been some ordeal.

I'm about out of news for this time. I'll try to write when I'm on R&R. Say "hi" to everyone for me, and tell Otis I got 105 days left. Write when you can.

Roger

During his R&R to Taiwan in the summer of 1968, Buchta fostered an interest in the principles of Buddhism when witnessing a Buddhist ceremony. He purchased this statue of Buddha during the trip and had it shipped home.

* * *

A few weeks would pass before the next communication home would reveal the soldier's current circumstances. Conversations that Buchta shared with his older brother in later years revealed a number of interesting details that transpired at Quang Tri, but which he chose not to place in any letters at the time of occurrence. In his earlier correspondence, the medic alluded to having to treat fellow service members who were engaging in prohibited sexual intercourse while on their R&R and other periods of leave. As Buchta once explained to his brother, many of these soldiers and Marines had been granted clearance to travel to Bangkok, often spending their money on women and wine, and, in the end, bringing home undesirable souvenirs that included a virtual litany of sexually transmitted diseases, such as gonorrhea. Once reporting back to their respective military bases following their off-duty escapades, theses soldiers would visit sick call at the hospital in an attempt to inconspicuously request that they be prescribed the appropriate antibiotics to treat the bacterial infections or other medical complications.

"Roger did mention a few times to me some details of the R&R he was able to take in Taiwan," said Don Buchta, reflecting on his younger brother's military service. "He and another guy spent about a week there, and he was able to attend a Buddhist ceremony, which he really found to be interesting. The experience seemed to inspire his later interest in the principles of Buddhism, and while he was in Taiwan, he purchased a statue of Buddha that he had shipped home."

On another occasion, Buchta experienced a moment that he never shared with his mother when he was off-duty at Quang Tri and lying on his cot in his tent reading a book. Any relaxation that he found in those moments quickly evaporated when he heard an enemy rocket hurtling toward his general location.

"The rocket struck outside the tent and the force of explosion threw Roger face first into a bookcase he had built from scrap wood," said Don. "It broke his nose, injured some of the bones in this face, and knocked out several of his teeth." He added, "After he got back from Vietnam, I remember that he went to the old VA hospital in Columbia and stayed there a couple of days while they reset his nose and did some work to correct the damage from the incident. Like he always said, if that rocket had hit any closer, he would have been killed."

As noted by the Military Order of the Purple Heart, the Purple Heart medal is a combat decoration "awarded to members of the armed forces of the U.S. who are wounded by an instrument of war in the hands of the enemy."[104] Buchta's injuries, which were caused by an enemy rocket, would have qualified him for receipt of the Purple Heart. However, being the withdrawn individual that he was while trying to forget his experiences in the war, in addition to lacking the necessary medical documentation that would verify his treatment for the wound while in Vietnam, Buchta chose to never pursue the venerated honor.

* * *

---

[104] The Military Order of the Purple Heart, *About the Military Order of the Purple Heart*, https://purpleheart.org.

Sp/4. Roger Buchta
542nd Medical Company
Quang Tri, South Vietnam
August 23, 1968

Dear Mom, Dad and Don:

The month of August is almost over. This month is really going past quickly. For me, that's a bit unusual considering the fact that I don't have much time left in this place. Usually, when guys get short, they begin watching the calendar, and time starts to drag. Maybe I'm not as time conscious as others. I don't know. Then, too, we have really been busy. The last two weeks the casualty rate has really been very high. Booby traps, ambushes, and accidents seem to be the villains. I'm not familiar with the statistics, but I would be willing to bet that one-third of our casualties in the last week are the result of miscalculations in air strikes, artillery strikes, and map reading. The other night, for instance, two rifle squads were on patrol when they were ambushed by their own men.; the result: one killed, six critically wounded, and eight seriously wounded. It is really puzzling sometimes.

Today we quit receiving patients and began evacuating the ones we had in preparation for our move next week. The hospital is supposed to be out of operation for about two weeks so that the inflatable units can be elevated on wooden floors and be re-arranged for the sake of convenience. It will be quite a job but also a change of pace, I think. Navy engineers are doing all the heavy work such as building floors, installing water mains, digging drainage ditches, etc. All we will have to do is move the structures and possibly sandbag if the Vietnamese don't do it. All the structures will be moved no more than fifty yards from our present location. Most of the equipment can be moved by hand…

I'm going to relate an incident that happened yesterday that you won't believe, but it's true. I saw two doctors carrying a litter with a dog on it to the operating room. I couldn't believe my eyes. The dog was a pet of one of the doctors and was in labor pains, unable to give birth. They called in the vet from across the street and our obstetrician. Four doctors performed a C-section on the dog. She had five pups, three of which were dead. A nurse who works in the operating room said a GI never received such treatment. The doctor to whom the dog belonged passed out cigars. He has the dog and its pups in a basket by his bunk. It could only happen in 'Nam.

That's about the extent of the news for this time. I've begun working evening shift (4-12) for the next week or so. As soon as they are through showing the evening's movie, we get the movie, projector, and speaker and show the movie at R&E. Tonight's a double feature—"Fort Utah" and "Reign of Terror"

(Sherlock Holmes mystery). Hope all of you are well.
Say "hi" to everyone for me and write soon.

Roger

* * *

September 28, 1968 was the date of the final letter that the medical specialist sent home from Quang Tri before his departure from Vietnam. Here he revealed that he had recently received a promotion to the new rank of Specialist Fifth Class. This new rank meant that Buchta was an "E-5" on the enlisted rank scale, receiving the same pay and benefits as a sergeant but was, in his medical position, focused on technical duties and not leading troops. The recently promoted soldier went on to explain that the inflatable units of the 18th Surgical Hospital had been moved and were almost at the point of being fully operational once again. The greatest concern now facing the soldier was to determine what items he would need to mail back home and which items he should carry on his person in a suitcase during his return flight to the states. His equipment and jungle fatigues would be turned into supply prior to leaving Vietnam, and many small items he had accumulated around his bunk area would either be sold to other soldiers remaining in Vietnam, given away, or discarded.

Three weeks earlier, on September 5th, the 542nd Medical Company received a call from the 67th Medical Group in Da Nang, Buchta explained, informing them that a typhoon was approaching the coast and heading inland in the direction of Quang Tri. The soldiers were, at the time, immersed in the process of moving the hospital and pieces had been strewn in several directions. Panic ensued while the soldiers scrambled to secure all of the various components lying exposed to the elements. It was fortunate that the warning was heeded, because later in the evening it began raining and poured for the next four days without pause. Fortune favored the hospital staff, and the associated winds caused little damage; however, the cool air it brought made sleeping much easier for the soldiers, who otherwise would have tossed and turned in the heat and humidity.

These military reflections quickly dissipated as Buchta's comments returned to the fact he would be leaving Vietnam in less than thirty days and would need someone to pick him up at the airport to give him a ride back home. A couple of weeks later, in the latter days of September 1968, Buchta turned in all of his assigned equipment at Da Nang and was approached by a retention non-commissioned officer about remaining in the Army. He was given the promise of a promotion and opportunity to remain at stateside bases to train other soldiers preparing to become medics in the Medical Corps. Prepared to return to his life back in rural Missouri, Buchta declined the offer and cleared through the 67th Medical Group in Da Nang before boarding a plane for Cam Ranh Bay along the southeastern coast of Vietnam. The plane then carried an elated Buchta home by way of Guam, Tokyo, and Anchorage, Alaska, before arriving at its final destination in the state of Washington. From there, Roger received his discharge at Fort Lewis and then boarded another airplane bound for St. Louis, where he was given a ride home from the airport from one of his uncles. According to his DD Form 214, the Report of Discharge, his final day as a soldier in Uncle Sam's military was October 13, 1966. For his service in the war, Roger was awarded the Vietnam Service Medal with an Overseas Service Bar.

"One of the first things that I remember him doing when he got home was going fishing in one of the big ponds on the property and catching two large catfish; it seems like he was more excited about that than anything else," related Don Buchta. "He then spent the next few months helping our father around the farm building fences and other such activities," he added. "In January [1969], he decided to return to Lincoln University and use his GI Bill to further his education and work toward earning his master's degree, so he could become a teacher."

Pausing, he concluded, "With all he had seen and experienced overseas, I never recall him criticizing the war… he was one of those guys that just chose not to share much about what happened over there. But years later, he would admit that he wished he had remained in the Army and made it a career out of it, even affirming that he would have gone back to Vietnam because it really was not all that bad of duty."

CHAPTER 10

Life as an Educator

"Unlike most ninth-graders in my school, I actually liked school. That's right. You heard me. I actually liked school, especially English and history. My teachers really seemed to care if I learned whatever I was supposed to learn." –Buchta wrote in his unpublished light horror novel titled "Satan's Mill."

Roger Dean Buchta was now prepared to place behind him the horrors of administering medical treatment to wounded troops in a heated combat zone. Instead, he embarked upon furthering his education through graduate school classes at Lincoln University. When he began classes in January 1969, Richard Milhous Nixon had only recently been sworn in to serve as the thirty-seventh president of the United States, having defeated Lyndon Johnson in the election weeks earlier. A World War II veteran of the U.S. Navy, President Nixon would, in the next few years of his presidency, end the country's involvement in the Vietnam War by entering into an accord with North Vietnam in early 1973.[105] During the same year the war in Vietnam came to a close, Nixon fulfilled a campaign promise made in 1968 to end the military draft, which had a few years earlier compelled Buchta into service with the U.S. Army during the war, and ushered the nation into an all-volunteer force.

During the summer commencement exercises held at Lincoln University in August 1971, Buchta was conferred a master's degree in education. He would apply for a position as librarian with his local school district, but he did not have the requisite classes to qualify for the position; however, in the summer of 1972, the announcement was made by the Russellville Board of Education that Buchta had been hired to begin teaching for the 1972-1973 school year. With his background and specific education, the district would now be able to add two levels of a foreign language class to their curriculum: German I and German II.[106] In the spring of 1974, Roger attended the Foreign Language Participation Day held at the

---

[105] The White House, *Richard M. Nixon*, www.whitehouse.gov.
[106] The August 6, 1972, edition of the *Sunday News and Tribune*.

University of Missouri in Columbia. He observed as students from different schools throughout the state competed in foreign language recitation, poetry, and skits. Students participating "were judged on intonation, pronunciation [and] the interpretation of the topic…"[107] Later the same year, when St. Paul's Lutheran Church in Lohman was celebrating the fiftieth anniversary of the construction of the current church building, both Roger and his brother, Don Buchta, shared their interest in history by researching much of the history of the church and sharing with the congregation a well-crafted slide-show following a worship service and basket dinner on October 27, 1974.[108]

Frances Engelbrecht, whom had taught Buchta as a sophomore in her language arts class during the 1959-1960 school year, later became a peer of her former student for two decades after he was hired by the school district. Her former student may have retained many of the characteristics he had possessed during high school, such as a quiet and often withdrawn demeanor; however, there were also some perceptible changes in his behavior that betrayed some of the stressful moments he had witnessed while serving as a medic in Vietnam.

"He wasn't the same Roger that I had taught in high school; you could sense there was an undercurrent of trauma that he had experienced," said Engelbrecht. "It seems like I can remember that his hands often trembled as well. I did not interact with him much because I was busy with so many student groups and other responsibilities in those days, but I sometimes saw him at lunch and recall

---

[107] May 5, 1974, edition of the *St. Joseph New-Press.*
[108] October 7, 1974, edition of the *Sunday News and Tribune.*

that he had a stellar vocabulary. Occasionally, he would speak up and use a word that I had never heard before, and I would have to go look it up in the dictionary"

This photo taken after returning from Vietnam shows Alma, Buchta's mother, holding their dog Otis. Buchta adored his canine friends and frequently inquired of them when writing home. Don Buchta recalls when his brother returned from Vietnam in October 1968, Otis paused for a moment in the doorway, then went "crazy" and bolted into the arms of his beloved friend.

She added, "The students would refer to him as 'Herr Buchta' because of his association with teaching German, and although he often appeared serious, he was very dedicated to his work, and I always thought he was a very good teacher that the students enjoyed."

His classroom was located on the southwest end of the school building in a basement room next to an area that had years earlier been used as the school's cafeteria. Situated away from the hustle and bustle of foot traffic, Buchta grew to appreciate his subterranean work abode. The private area afforded him opportunities to quietly slip out a nearby side door between classes and engage in his decades-long habit of smoking cigarettes away from the judgmental eyes of his students. In addition to the classes in German Roger was instructing, he later added sociology, world history, American history, geography, and economics classes to his teaching repertoire. In 1974, at the encouragement of then Superintendent Grover Snead, he established "Der Deutsche Verein," (the German Association), which later became known simply as the "German Club."

A lifelong bachelor, Buchta briefly dated a young woman, a fellow teacher who instructed art classes, during the early part of his tenure at Russellville High School. During their short period of social engagement, he even took his female friend to see a show put on by country music icon Roy Clark at the Lake of the Ozarks. However, as his older brother remarked, the former soldier had the ability to easily become "bored" with individuals who did not share many common interests, and Roger chose to remain single, dedicating his time to fishing, woodworking, and gardening.

"He always lived at home with our parents because he loved the outdoors, and he could walk all over the property, or go down to the river and climb the bluffs for recreation," explained Don Buchta. "He simply loved being outside. Roger was very agile and could climb the bluffs like some kind of animal," he chuckled. "But, one interest that changed for him was hunting, which he loved to do before the war. Not long after he got home from Vietnam, he quit hunting all at once—he said that he had witnessed enough killing and after that, he never picked up a gun again."

When Buchta applied for the librarian vacancy at Russellville High School in 1972, and was instead hired as a teacher, the woman who was offered the librarian job, Jo Ann Sullivan, would become a close friend. Sullivan moved to Missouri after her husband, Billie, was discharged from the United States Air Force, and the couple found a small farm to purchase.[109] She would serve as the librar-

---

[109] Billie R. Sullivan served a total of thirty-five years in the military between the U.S. Air Force, Arizona National Guard, Air Force Reserve and Missouri

ian for Russellville High School until retiring in 1996. Recalling her friend's uniqueness, sense of humor, and seemingly boundless knowledge of history, Sullivan explained that Buchta was, in her observation, a fantastic teacher whose dedication and knowledge helped many students, particularly one very close to her.

"My daughter had him as a teacher in many of her classes at Russellville, and when she applied for college in Warrensburg, she had been instilled with such a range of knowledge by Mr. Buchta, that she was able to test out of several history and liberal arts classes."

Sullivan noted that sometime in the early 1990s, Buchta passed out at school, and it was soon discovered that he had experienced a hypoglycemic episode. He soon began taking protein supplements every few hours and snacking throughout the day, which seemed to "take care of it," she recalled.

She continued, "I remember he took up crafting back when he was teaching and bought some kind of wood jigsaw for that purpose. He made me a beautiful, detailed wall hanging that I still have and treasure to this day."

On more than one occasion, Buchta and Sullivan, in addition to other teachers and staff at the school in Russellville, volunteered to serve as chaperones for groups of high school students on trips to Europe in the summer months. Both the students and staff had to cover their own expenses related to the trip. Many memorable moments arose from these overseas journeys, but Sullivan recalls a

---

National Guard. In his civilian endeavors, he was employed by the Missouri Department of Corrections for more than twenty-five years, most recently as associate superintendent of the Boonville Correctional Center. June 13, 2019, edition of the *Boonville Daily News*.

distinct circumstance related to her friend's knowledge of the German language.

"We arrived in one little town in Germany early one evening, and I remember that some of us went to a little German café—or whatever they were called over there," she said. "Roger did all of the reading on the menus because he was so well educated in the German language, but he refused to speak to the waiters in German because he didn't think his accent was good enough to do so," she added.

Sharon Easter was hired by the Russellville School District in 1971 as the Home Economics teacher. After Buchta was hired the following year, the two soon became friends, visiting frequently throughout the school day outside of her classroom,

Buchta was at times a passive rebel, quietly refusing to comport with socially-accepted norms. He is pictured in a relaxed manner in his official yearbook photograph from 1976, displaying an open-collared shirt and a loosened tie.

adjacent to the high school principal's office and next door to their colleague, Frances Engelbrecht. In 1999, both Easter and Buchta chose to retire at the end of the school year.

"He was just an easygoing person," recalled Easter. "I would also describe him as a pleasant gentleman who was comfortable to be around, and I think the students really liked him because he was a good teacher."

She added, "He never talked much about Vietnam, and it was several years after we began working together that I even learned that he was a veteran. He talked about being a member of the Sierra Club because of the way they worked to protect wildlife and the forests. We both loved the Westminster (Kennel Club) Dog Show, but neither of us could seem to keep track of when it was going to be televised, so, if one of us got home and saw that it was going to be on, we would call the other."

Another lighthearted reflection is tied to the aforementioned period when Buchta experienced some challenges in regulating his blood sugar, and she remained by his side to provide a little support and encouragement.

"One day I saw him leaning against the senior lockers outside of my classroom, and he was kind of loopy, not feeling well at all," she explained. "He had already called his brother to come pick him up. I tried to get him to come into my classroom and sit down because the bell was going to ring in about fifteen minutes, and the students would be swarming the hallways.

Pausing, she continued, "He said that he just had to sit down, pressed his shoulders against the lockers and slid to the floor. Since I couldn't convince him to get up and come into my classroom, I slid down beside him and just sat there until his brother arrived. When the bell rang, all the students walked by and just looked over at the two teachers sitting on the hallway floor, but not a one of them said a word to us," she laughed.

While getting to know Buchta, as they continued to work together, one of her friend's greatest traits that she grew to appreciate was his dry wit and intelligent sense of humor, which, she explained, could make her chuckle and lighten the mood even during difficult moments.

Based upon suggestion and encouragement from Superintendent Grover Snead, Buchta, far right, established "Der Deutsche Verein," (the German Association), which later became known simply as the German Club at Russellville High School in 1974.

"I can recall a time when we were both in the principal's outer office at the end of the school quarter, and I was griping because I didn't think I could get all of my grading done by Monday. He looked at me and flatly said, "Just give them a letter grade because you know what they were going to make from the beginning of the school year." Grinning, she added, "He was kidding, of course, but his humor sure made me feel better."

In the 1980s, Buchta became a member of the Russellville Lions Club and, despite his quiet and often reserved nature, rose to the position of president of the organization. When the organization began to extend membership to women in 1987, Jo Ann

Sullivan recalled that her friend was very influential in convincing her to become a member. The Lions Club legacy in the Russellville community dates back to November 22, 1949, when it was granted its charter with thirty-eight members. In the early years, the Lions hosted such events as rodeos and horse shows, while pancake suppers and ham and bean suppers became their primary source of income in later years. Their efforts have been a boon to the community and have supported such initiatives as the formation of the volunteer fire department, the establishment of the city's water works, and construction of senior housing and ball fields. This institution also possesses a leading role in the annual Christmas parade. In 1988, when the community of Russellville celebrated their sesquicentennial over a period of three days, June 10-12, Buchta, who was serving as the organization's president, offered as part of his responsibilities, the welcoming remarks during the celebration.[110]

When his father, William, passed away in 1983, he had willed to his two sons and his wife sections of the farm on which they had lived and worked for decades. However, as Don Buchta explained, there were some complications with the structure of their father's will, and both he and his brother had to purchase the land that was supposed to have been given to them. Ten years later, when their mother entered eternal rest, the remaining sections of the farm were passed down to her sons without any legal difficulties. For a few years, Don would bale hay on his property. but when other demands on his time emerged, he and Roger chose to rent out the property to be farmed by others.

---

[110] Raithel, *Russellville, Mo. Sesquicentennial: 1838-1988*, 123-124.

Three years after Buchta began teaching at Russellville High School, David Russell was hired to fulfill the role of Industrial Arts teacher after his predecessor, Jerome Eggers, died from injuries sustained in an automobile accident in November 1975.[111] Russell explained that he and Buchta quickly developed a friendship since, as he recalled, they were at the time the only single male teachers working in the high school, and neither of them enjoyed being in large crowds of people. In the early years of teaching at the school, David

noted that he, and his fellow teacher, helped run an after-school gymnastics program for kids in the cafeteria. Additionally, their friendship expanded to include activities outside of regular school activities.

"We seemed to hit if off right away, and we visited quite a bit during the school day," said Russell. "He would come down to my shop class during the school day, and I think that's where he might have caught some of the interest that he developed in woodworking

While on a fishing trip to the Lake of the Ozarks in the early 1980s, David Russell caught this sixty-one-pound spoonbill. Buchta was one of the teachers on the trip that held onto Russell as he struggled to pull the monstrous fish onto the dock.

---

[111] Born in Jefferson City, Missouri on March 18, 1948, Jerome Allen Eggers was only twenty-seven years old when he died on November 26, 1975, from injuries sustained in an automobile accident four days earlier. He was laid to rest in Riverview Cemetery in Jefferson City.

years later. We both liked to fish, and I would hang out with him and his brother at their farm on and off for several years." Chuckling, he added, "I can remember going down to the creek at Roger's place to fish, smoke some cigarettes, and drink a little beer, but I never seemed to catch anything."

In the early 1980s, Russell recalled, many of the male teachers and administrative staff would celebrate the end of the school year by taking a fishing trip down to the Lake of the Ozarks. One of these trips, a rather large fish was pulled in by Russell while Buchta and a couple of others held onto the angler to prevent him from being pulled into the water.

"I was using just a basic Zebco rod and reel—nothing fancy— and managed to catch a sixty-one-pound spoonbill," he excitedly explained. "Roger convinced me to take it by the Department of Conservation, and I got a master angler award for it." He added, "Then, we took the fish over to Roger's, and he helped me clean it."

In the early 1980s, when the basketball team for Russellville was enjoying an impressive winning streak, Russell often joined Buchta and his brother to watch the games and to cheer them on as they played other schools throughout mid-Missouri. Additionally, he and Buchta joined other teachers on float trips during the summer months.

"He really liked to observe the players and support the kids at the school," Russell affirmed.

Maribeth Lupardus was hired at Russellville High School in 1985, to teach an assortment of business courses such as typing, accounting, and shorthand. The following year, she and David Russell married and, although the couple remained friends with

Buchta, the demands of continuing to work full-time at the school and raising three children took precedence.

"Roger had a heart of gold and a great sense of humor," said Maribeth Russell.

Her husband added, "He liked having his classroom in the basement of the school because of the privacy it provided, and this way he could make his way out one of the side doors and smoke between classes. There was one year that they moved his classroom upstairs for some reason, and he didn't like that at all. The next year, he was able to convince administration to let him move back down to the basement."

Pausing in mirthful reflection, Russell concluded, "One interesting thing about him that I remember is that he always seemed to be very particular about his coffee—he would only drink it out of a china cup, and that's what he kept in his classroom. He was a different type of guy with his own unique habits, but he was always a good friend to me."

When discussing Buchta's romantic interests during the time he taught at Russellville, Russell added, "He dated some... and was very attracted to blondes, I remember." He sagely concluded, "But sometimes, you just don't meet the right person."

Two years after Buchta was hired, Jana Thompson joined the staff at Russellville and went on to fulfill a medley of roles during her employment, which included teaching first, second, and fourth grades, special education, special reading, curriculum director, and acting as assistant principal for kindergarten through eighth grades. In her early years with the school system, she first came to know Buchta when she encountered him in the teacher's break room located off the east end of the school cafeteria, which, at the time, was the only indoor location where teachers were allowed to smoke.

"Roger would be there in the mornings or during his breaks getting his coffee, and that's where we began to visit and where I first got to know him," said Thompson.

She went on to explain that a few years later, she joined Buchta, David Russell, and the former principal, Jack Brumley, in running the afterschool gymnastics program for the children.

"At the time, I was kind of in charge of the program because I had been a cheerleader in school and participated in synchronized swimming when I was younger," she recalled. "I remember Roger had done gymnastics at some point in his life and got on the parallel bars and began demonstrating a few swings and moves that really impressed us. He was strong and very agile," she added.

Many years later, Thompson's son, Ben, not only became a student of his mother's former teaching colleague, but helped breathe renewed life into a revered piece of farm equipment that had been in the Buchta family for many decades. Ben Thompson planned to participate in the 2000 Chevron Lubricants Tractor Restoration Competition as part of a Future Farmers of America project and discovered that Buchta had a 1952 John Deere MT that had been used by his father. Sadly, the tractor had sat in a barn for a number of years and was no longer operable because of mechanical concerns that develop with time. As part of the competition, young Thompson was granted the opportunity to restore the tractor. During the process, he was informed that the tractor had been used by William Buchta for projects around the farm such as mowing, cultivating, and sundry other chores, and the late farmer's sons now wished to have it available for mowing around the property, pulling a trailer, and possibly driving in parades. Ben labored untold hours working on the tractor and eventually won a national award for the restoration.

Kay Kasiske invested a number of years as a substitute teacher at the junior high and high school level at Russellville prior to being hired in a full-time capacity. During her tenure at the school, she instructed such classes as Language Arts, Journalism, Newspaper, and Yearbook. Through her recollection, she and Buchta always seemed to get along well and shared many common interests. On one occasion, when the school librarian suggested to several of the teachers and members of the administrative staff that they should consider chaperoning student trips to Europe, Kasiske volunteered to participate in two separate summer trips. She recalls the excitement Buchta revealed when visiting locations throughout Europe, especially Germany. However, although he appreciated witnessing such historic sites as the Brandenburg Gate and viewing the Berlin Wall, traveling into East Germany raised some concern for the educator and German historian.

"On one of these trips, I believe it was back in 1987, our bus was getting ready to enter into East Berlin through Checkpoint Charlie," said Kasiske.[112] "A lot of the students were joking around and acting like young people do sometimes, and I remember Roger becoming worried and saying the kids need to behave—there's Stasi guards up there.[113] We watched the bus in front of us; when the Stasi guards

---

[112] Checkpoint Charlie was the third checkpoint opened by Allied forces in the vicinity of Berlin and "became the most famous crossing point between East and West Germany." It has a storied Cold War history and now serves as an important tourist destination for those visiting in Berlin. Visit Berlin, *Checkpoint Charlie*, https://visitberlin.de/en.

[113] The Ministry for State Security, otherwise known as the "Stasi," were the secret police established in East Germany in 1950. Organized along military

boarded, the kids sat up straight and were well-behaved." She added, "When it was our turn to go through and the Stasi boarded our bus, the students were well behaved, too."

Although her friend and former colleague, Kasiske recalled, was focused on ensuring his students received a quality education, there was a certain occasion when he discovered that his lecture-style delivery method created challenges for one student in particular.

"From what I remember Roger telling me, there was a certain student in one of his classes that always seemed to be falling asleep during class," said Kasiske. Apparently, Roger was so frustrated with the student that he was prepared to fail him. It is my understanding that this student really needed to pass the class in order to graduate. The boy's mother came to school to see what could be done, and the agreement was made that if she would sit in class with her son and ensure that he stayed awake and paid attention, then Roger would pass him. On the third day of doing this, Roger looked over while lecturing and saw that both the boy and his mother had fallen asleep," she chuckled. "Well, Roger passed the student but was also able to make his point that he was serious about teaching—that there were specific things he wanted this student to understand in addition to being attentive while in his class."

Donita Stubinger, a Lohman resident who attended church with Buchta, shed additional light upon the aforementioned story.

---

lines similar in structure to the Soviet secret police, the Stasi were both feared and hated, and were known for their aggressiveness and brutality, many times making arbitrary arrests. The Stasi worked at Checkpoint Charlie conducting passport controls and vetting individuals entering and leaving East Germany during the height of the Cold War. They were formally disbanded in 1990 in the months the fall of the Berlin Wall.

She recalled, "I was told by my son, Craig, that I had to go to a parent-teacher conference for his history class taught by Mr. Buchta. My son is an outdoor type of guy and could work all hours of the day and night—school was the least of his worries at this time. He needed the history credit to graduate, and while I was discussing his situation with Mr. Buchta, I was advised that if Craig would stay awake in his class and quit sleeping, he would consider passing him."

Stubinger then made the remark to her son's teacher: "What would you have me do to keep him awake? Come sit by him and punch him as he falls asleep?" To her surprise, Buchta flatly replied, "I'll get you a chair."

Soon, she was making arrangements to leave work during her lunch hour to drive from Jefferson City to Russellville to sit alongside her son in his history class. Upon her arrival on the first day, just as promised, a chair was waiting for her. For some time, every Monday through Friday, Stubinger continued to make the trip in an effort to keep her son awake and make sure he earned the necessary credit to graduate.

"I never did care much for history, and during one of these classes I fell asleep," she recalled. "I woke up to the sound of the entire class laughing at me. For the rest of the semester, I made sure that I had something to do during the class, whether it was paying bills or writing Christmas cards. Essentially, I did anything I could to stay busy because I never wanted to fall asleep in his class again!"

Chuckling, she concluded, "Craig passed the class and graduated. We never discussed Craig sleeping in his class again, and we sure didn't discuss me coming to his class. I never did tell Mr. Buchta thank you, but he was a great history teacher."

Many of Buchta's former students were first introduced to the educator's unwavering love for animals through his declared "oversights" during slideshow presentations in the classroom. Oftentimes, Buchta would set up a carousel projector to share photographs with his various classes, oftentimes inserting a photograph of his dog Daisy, a Pomeranian, into the grouping. When the carousel came to one of the slides showing Daisy, the teacher would innocently remark, "Oh, how did that get in there?" Other times, Buchta would reveal his renowned agility during lectures when standing in front of the class with one leg bent upward with his foot hiked upon the top of his desk with his other foot on the ground and a hand in his pocket. On other occasions, his uniqueness was revealed when students entering the classroom before the bell rang only to observe their teacher sitting atop a four-drawer filing cabinet with his legs crossed while reading a book.

As one of the sponsors for the Class of 1987, Buchta took part in the class photographs used in the school yearbook. When showing up unprepared for the photo session, one of his students, Joe Jobe, loaned him a gray jacket to wear in the photograph.

There are a number of former students who also recall when the educator taught them a handful of German songs in their German classes—such as "Oh Tannenbaum" around Christmastime—in addition to providing demonstrations of unique dances including waltzes and the lighthearted "ducky-dance."

Despite his open-mindedness and irreverent responses to many happenings in the world around him, Buchta was also very set in his ways about certain personal activities and interests—such as his smoking habit. When the campus of Russellville schools was declared to be non-smoking during his tenure there, he affirmed that he would smoke wherever he pleased regardless of any arbitrary prohibitions implemented by administrators and the school board. There were only the barely perceptible flakes of cigarette ashes outside the side door near his basement classroom to serve as a testament to his stubbornness and eschewing of rules that he viewed as ridiculous.

When Joe Jobe entered high school at Russellville as a freshman in 1983, his earliest introduction to Roger Buchta was when the teacher was assigned as one of his class sponsors. Sponsors were assigned to a specific class at the beginning of their freshman year and remained as supporters of the class through the end of their senior year and graduation. As part of the sponsor's duties, they would help guide the students during class meetings and assist with the election of their class officers each year. Additionally, the class sponsors assisted with fundraising events such as those associated with the annual school carnival, the funds of which were then used to host celebrated activities including the school prom. In years past, noted Buchta's fellow teacher, Sharon Easter, the sophomore class at Russellville High School inherited the responsibility of serving the dinner at the prom, and the sponsors would have assisted in the activity. Not all of the duties of the sponsors were stressful and demanding, however, since they also accompanied the students on their senior trip, which generally included a few days at the Missouri vacation destinations of either Branson or the Lake of the Ozarks.

In the early weeks of 1987, as the senior class was preparing for their approaching graduation by waiting in line to have their senior photographs taken for the school yearbook, Buchta's unpreparedness left Joe Jobe with a mirthful memory of his former teacher.

"Since he was one of the class sponsors, he got his photograph taken as well," recalled Jobe. "He was in line in front of me and said, 'Damn it, Joe, I forgot it was picture day. I didn't wear anything good.' I said, 'Here, put on my jacket,' and that's the one he was wearing in the photograph," Jobe laughed. "He didn't care about how he looked in the photo because it wasn't his graduation."

In his duties as the sponsor of the senior class, Buchta, along with the students, provided a quote that was printed in the yearbook. Summoning his wit and intellect, he advised the students, "Keep one eye on the past and one on the future," calling upon his experience as a teacher of world history by invoking the memory of Janus, the god of beginnings and transitions in Roman mythology, who is generally depicted as having two faces looking in opposite directions.

One habit that never came to mind when describing Buchta was lavish spending. Roger was known to save most of the money he earned while he and his brother continued to live in the house where they were raised. Jobe recalls that one comment made by his former teacher validated Buchta's unadorned, thrifty views on living in a world inclined to frivolity and waste.

"We were in our economics class, shortly before the bell rang and class began, and there was a conversation going on between some of my classmates in the front of the class," said Jobe. "Some were complaining about how many times they had to move in their lives while others were complaining about having to live in the same house for so long. Herr Buchta listened and then polished off the conversation with a mic drop— 'How about this one,' he said. 'I slept in the same bed that I was born in... until last year. I finally threw it out!'"

The daily routine of teaching classes—specifically those related to history—never prevailed in diminishing his enthusiasm for the subject, in part due to the ever changing and evolving moments related to the Cold War during which he had come of age. Years earlier, Buchta had watched the transformation that came with the construction of the Berlin Wall. "The fall of the Berlin Wall, like its construction, took place in a single night. Just as on 13 August 1961, a city and a people awoke to find themselves divided, so on the morning of 10 November 1989 that division was no more," explained Frederick Taylor in his fascinating book *The Berlin Wall: A World Divided, 1961-1989*.[114] Having grown into adulthood during many momentous occurrences of the Cold War, Buchta, ever the devoted teacher of history, remained transfixed for days to the televised coverage of the wall coming down. He was enthralled as he witnessed history being written while stressing to his students the importance of understanding and remembering such a historic event as the one that was unfolding before their own eyes.

A little more than two years later, another unforgettable event for children of the Cold War transpired with the resignation of Soviet president Mikhail Gorbachev on Christmas Day 1991. This change heralded the collapse of the Soviet Union. Born in a small Russian village to a peasant family, Gorbachev grew critical of the inefficiencies of the "Soviet System" at a young age and would go on to be elected General Secretary of the Communist Party of the Soviet Union in 1985; four years later he was elected President of the Soviet

---

[114] Taylor, *The Berlin Wall*, 429.

Union by the new parliament.[115] In 1990, he was awarded the Nobel Peace Prize for his role in bringing greater peace to the world through the ending of the Cold War. He remained active after leaving politics and in 1993 became founding president of Green Cross International—"an international independent environmental organization" that advocates "for environmental and developmental sustainability in the face of threats posed by over consumption and use of fossil fuels, development of nuclear technology and growing gap between rich and poor."[116]

Sharing an interest with Gorbachev in matters related to environmental protections and realizing the momentous achievement of ending the Cold War, Buchta provided some incentive to his students to witness the former Soviet president speak in person. On May 6, 1992, Gorbachev visited Westminster College in Fulton, Missouri, where forty-six years earlier, Winston Churchill, in the presence of Missouri-born President Harry S. Truman, delivered his famous speech titled "The

Don, left, and Roger Buchta are pictured in St. Paul's Lutheran Church Cemetery in 2014 next to the graves of two German immigrants shot and killed by Confederate troops in the Civil War. In their retirement, the brothers traveled and performed research together pertaining to items of local historical interest.

---

[115] The Nobel Prize, *Mikhail Gorbachev*, https://nobelprize.org.
[116] Green Cross International, *Mikhail Gorbachev*, https://gcint.org.

Sinews of Peace," a stark warning of growing Soviet influence in Europe and embracing the metaphor of the "iron curtain" in describing the threat of the spread of communism. With the former Soviet president visiting the same college in Missouri that hosted Churchill decades earlier, Buchta offered to award extra credit to the students in his history classes if they attended Gorbachev's speech. A reported 20,000 people gathered on the campus of the college to listen to Gorbachev deliver his forty-five-minute speech behind the same podium used by Churchill decades earlier. As noted by the National Churchill Museum, located on the campus of Westminster College, the former Soviet president's speech "brought Westminster and the world full circle—proclaiming an end to the Cold War and the beginning of a new era holding the promise of peace."[117] Additional historical irony emerges from the location of Gorbachev's speech, which took place in front of Edwina Sandys' *Breakthrough* sculpture made from eight original sections of the Berlin Wall.

In 1993, ten years after the death of his father, Buchta's mother, Alma, passed away and was laid to rest in the cemetery of St. Paul's Lutheran Church in Lohman, where she had been a member her entire life. Shortly after her passing, Buchta settled on the decision to build an A-Frame structure adjacent to the house where he had grown up and which continued to serve as the residence for both he and his older brother. The inspiration for the A-Frame structure, some assert, came from seeing the home of a fellow teacher who once resided in such a unique architectural structure. Others claim Roger fell in love with the home design after having witnessed such

---

[117] The National Churchill Museum, *Mikhail Gorbachev 5/6/92*, https://national-churchillmuseum.org.

structures nestled in the forested mountainsides throughout many European locations.

"When he was first thinking about building the A-Frame, he said that it was so he would have a house he could smoke inside," said long-time colleague, Sharon Easter. "He lived in his mother's house—and he always referred to it as his mother's house—and he wasn't going to smoke in there out of respect for her, even after she passed."

She added, "He asked if I would draw him a floor plan for the A-Frame because I was always good at that type of thing, and I believe those are the plans that he used when he had it built."

Don Buchta explained that his brother continued to refine and improve his woodworking skills, purchasing all the tools and equipment needed for numerous types of intricate projects. When construction of the A-Frame was completed, he built cabinets for the structure in addition to a beautifully-crafted wet bar. Throughout the years, they hosted a number of gatherings at their auxiliary home, including poker games, playing pool, and associated recreational activities. One of the events that Roger both enjoyed hosting and participating in was Halloween, possibly because it provided him an outlet to conceal with a costume his usual reserved self and present himself as another character in an alternative world.

The years continued their unrelenting grind forward, and as the late 1990s approached, a bond issue was passed by voters to allow for the construction of a new campus on the western edge of Russellville that initially served as the junior high in 1998. However, the school board decided they were going to prepare to shift the new campus into the high school, which would then require Buchta, a high-school level teacher, to depart his familiar and comfortable basement surroundings and move his classroom to the newer facility. His heart and soul, many former colleagues remarked, was invested at the older of the two school campuses. This, along with the fact that his older brother had already entered retirement, motivated his decision to himself retire in 1999, after having accrued twenty-seven years as an educator. As part of this retirement and in recognition for his years of service to the school, he received a dinner and a small plaque that for years hung inconspicuously in the living room of his mother's home.

Once leaving his teaching career, Roger truly became more of a hermit, spending a greater amount of time at home investing countless hours in woodworking, walking, kayaking, and exploring sites of local historic interest in the company of his brother. As Don Buchta explained, they were also able to make several trips overseas, such as one made to Egypt, where they spent nearly three weeks and enjoyed a cruise down the Nile River.

Buchta had this A-Frame constructed in 1993 to provide him a place to smoke indoors and to also serve as a location to occasionally entertain family and friends. In evenings, he would come here to watch television, read and write.

"Roger was always a great travel partner, and it seems like we went somewhere about every summer—Germany, Austria, Switzerland… several countries," said Don Buchta. "He did his research on most of the places we went and knew much about every location we visited. He also never seemed to get tired."

The love of travel cultivated by Buchta in his later years did not include the operation of automobiles, his older brother explained. In the late 1980s, Buchta was driving his brother's new Ford Mustang to school early one morning when a teenager, who was racing through town in his own vehicle, collided with the car Buchta was driving near Russellville city limits. The airbags deployed in the Mustang, likely preventing the teacher from suffering any serious physical injuries, and he was back at work the next day. Emotionally shaken by the incident, in the years that followed, Buchta would drive himself to school and then back home, but he soon came to rely upon his brother for transportation to anywhere of any appreciable distance.

His older brother also noted that when Roger was not fishing or engaged in some other form of outdoor activity that he dearly enjoyed, he became quite adept at plumbing and electrical work, completing associated projects around their house and farm when need arose. Additionally, he was very meticulous in his woodworking and constructed several "state of the art" projects such as a grandfather clock, mantle clocks, and detailed miniature representations of his grandmother's home, and a Victorian house that were prominently displayed inside the A-Frame.

Although he enjoyed researching local history in the company of his older brother, Buchta leveraged a large part of his own historical knowledge and experiences to write a number of lengthy novels. Roger used his literary talents to explore the genres of horror, fantasy, and science-fiction genre; many of these novels spanned three to four-hundred pages in length. Although the books were detailed, creative, and well-written, Buchta would only on rare occasion allow close friends to read the works and demonstrated no desire to ever have the works published or share them to any greater extent. In one self-published work, *Satan's Mill*, his writings, though presented in a fictional context, appear to be a reflection of both his experiences and interests as a student in addition to his self-appraised role as a teacher in delivering a good education in his classes.

"Unlike most ninth-graders in my school, I actually liked school," he wrote. "That's right. You heard me. I actually liked school, especially English and history. My teachers really seemed to care if I learned whatever I was supposed to learn."

By the time he had reached seventy years of age, there was a perceptible deterioration in Buchta's health brought on by years of smoking—a habit that began in his high school years. He appeared much frailer, walking with a perceptible lean in his gait, and occasionally paused in his step because of his troubled and often labored breathing. Woefully, he had reached a time when he was no longer able to traverse any appreciable distance nor participate in most of the other outdoor activities he had embraced in earlier years. In 2017, recognizing their own mortality, he and his brother purchased headstones decorated with their unique interests and personality, having them placed in the cemetery of St. Paul's Lutheran Church in Lohman, adjacent to the gravesite of their parents. It was a moment in the wisp of one's life that most attempt to ignore or delay, but as a single man with no heirs, Buchta was making preparations for the next and final journey of his existence—his inevitable passing.

EPILOGUE

A creature of habit may have become an obsolescent phrase in local lexicon, but it is certainly one that came to define Roger Buchta in his twilight years. A good number of days, when the weather was comfortable and inviting in the spring and summer months, he found enjoyment by remaining outdoors during the daylight hours to garden and plant various types of flowers and shrubs in decorative beds. In the evenings, it became his custom to amble over to the A-Frame to smoke his cigarettes, watch a few television programs, or work on researching and writing novels that would never be formally published. When he was finished, Roger would walk the few steps back to his "mother's house," drink two Miller High Life beers, eat a bowl of cereal, and stay up to watch a little more television while visiting with his brother. He would finally traverse the steps to his upstairs bedroom and lie down sometime around 12:30 or 1:00 a.m.

The day of February 4, 2019 was like many others. The retired teacher did a little work outside of the house. When evening approached, he slipped out of the house and walked over to the A-Frame, where he spent several hours engaged in the assortment of solitary activities he had come to enjoy. When the hands of the clock began to approach midnight, Roger walked the short distance back to the house, consumed his two beers and bowl of cereal, petted his Pomeranian, Harry, and visited with his brother.

"He watched television until about 1:00 a.m. or so, and, as far as I could tell, nothing seemed out of the ordinary," recalled his older brother, Don. "When he went up to go to bed, it's almost like he knew he was going to pass away because he laid out on his desk some M-16 shells he had brought back from Vietnam and some medals he had earned over there," he added.

The next morning, Don rose from bed and a short while later noticed that his brother was not yet out of bed. When he walked up the stairs to check on him, he found Roger lying face down on the floor near the top of the steps. Rolling him over, he began to perform chest compressions in an effort to revive him. A few minutes later, when his revival attempts proved unsuccessful, Don bolted down the stairs to call emergency services. Upon reaching the house, the paramedics made every attempt to revive Roger, which proved to be fruitless.

"I think that he must have felt that a heart attack was coming on and got out of bed sometime during the night... and that's when he fell," said Don, lowering his head in pained reflection.

Roger's dog, Harry, whom he had doted over and pampered just as he had every other dog he had ever owned, was known to frequently scurry up the steps and look around his former master's room for months after his death, wagging his tale in hopes that he might have returned in his absence.

Friends, family, fellow educators, former students, and those with whom Buchta attended church gathered at a funeral home in Russellville on the evening of February 8, 2019, to pay their final respects in front of the closed casket draped with the flag of the country he had served under in Vietnam decades earlier. The following morning, Roger's funeral was held in the St. Paul's Lutheran Church, where he had attended with his parents and remained a member his entire life, although his attendance at services had declined in the years following the war.

"I would often ask him if he wanted to go to worship services on Sundays with me but rarely would he go after he returned from Vietnam," remarked Don Buchta. "It seemed as if he had lost interest, but when it came to religious history, he knew more than most any preacher or religious leader did."

Though rarely discussing and never boasting about his military experiences during the war, Buchta was then laid to rest in the cemetery behind the "Church on the Hill," in a plot adjacent to his parents with full military honors rendered by volunteers from the local Veterans of Foreign Wars post and members of the Missouri National Guard funeral honors team.

The harsh lessons in wounds and death he received in Vietnam ensured that he would never be a person supportive of war; instead, Roger choose to remain separated from his brothers and sisters who were active in their support of veteran's organizations. For him, such associations would bring back memories of the atrocities he had witnessed and had assiduously struggled to suppress in his own mind. He made the decision to invest his emotional strength to matters of academia—continuing his life of learning, doting over the numerous animals around the farm, gaining a deeper appreciation of classical music all while refining what became more than a modicum of talent in woodworking.

The headstone he had purchased a couple years previous, in obvious preparation for what he realized to be his inevitable passing, denotes his enduring interest in the German language and includes a proclamation that affirms his love and adoration for members of the animal kingdom. Below an inscribed picture of his dog, Harry, and one of the many cats that could be seen scrambling around the farm, a statement written in German upon his headstone reads, "UNSERE TIERLIEBE ERHEBT UNS AUS DEM ABGRUND DER BARBAREI ZU DEN HÖHEN DER HÖFLICHKEIT." (*Our love of animals elevates us from the abyss of barbarism to the height of courtesy.*)

"Roger was a loner, didn't mix much with others, and pretty much kept to himself all of the time, but he certainly wasn't an irritable individual either," said his brother. "His life is a collection of fascinating stories that includes his time in Vietnam and being over there and present for the Tet Offensive." With a notable pause, he added, "I have attended four different colleges and universities in my life and had some great instructors, but I can assure you that not one of them had as much real-life experience or were as intelligent as Roger was."

Never boasting of his time in the service, Buchta spent decades trying to silence the visage of the horrors he witnessed as a medic in the war, images of

Prior to his passing, Buchta had a personalized headstone installed in the cemetery of St. Paul's Lutheran Church in Lohman. In addition to phrases written in German, it features etches of his dog, Harry, and a cat from their farm.

young men cut down in their prime and having to be sent home in the inauspicious collections of plain body bags. He silently suffered through any inner struggles, hesitant to publicly bare his emotions; rather, he focused on his career as an educator and later invested his emotional output into such hobbies as crafting grandfather clocks and other hobby projects. Few would grow close to the former soldier or come to know him on a deep, passionate level. He found his release in the process of writing, through which he was able to express his desires and interests absent the complications that come with building complex interpersonal relationships or subjecting oneself to the potential judgment of others.

Through the many unpublished books, articles, and other written works that he left behind, Roger shared his understanding and interests in subjects ranging from history to science fiction and dabbled in the genre of light horror, exploring a host of delicate and socially-sensitive topics to include human sexuality. The countless hours he would invest in his writings demonstrated a morsel of the boundless creativity he possessed, and his ability to weave engaging plots in novels such as *Winsome Witches* and *Satan's Mill*. Within many of these unique works, Buchta reveals an abundance of insight into, not only the varied impulses that inspire and motivate individuals, but lays bare his appreciation for the endurance and strength of the human spirit. His writings, much of which were molded around some of his own personal experiences and beliefs, were structured into threads of beautifully crafted narratives that express the gift of hope in the most trying of circumstances. Some of his prose demonstrates the potential to buoy even the most depressed of minds and expose his belief that any struggles he may have been subjected to while winding his way across the mortal realm would be replaced by better days to come. These words emanating from his pen became a positive testament to those willing to silence their cluttered thoughts and absorb the promise of peace that arrives upon one's passing from the earth, no longer suffering from the horrors of war or bodies ravaged by ill-health and time. Buchta has since passed on, but through his literary endeavors, some of what he left after his departure include a cloaked message affirming that the end of one's life was an event not to be feared or regretted.

"Out of this darkness… a new and better world will emerge," he presciently penned only a few years before his passing. "We shall pass through this darkness and eventually step out onto sunlit meadows of green and gold. Have faith, my friends, have faith. Better days are on the horizon."

Many of his writings pay homage to the frontiers of dreams and have become an enduring link to the interest Buchta possessed in the founder of psychoanalysis, Sigmund Freud. In many of his classes, the educator often spoke about the work of the Austrian neurologist and his efforts in peeling away the layers of the human brain through psychoanalysis and the interpretation of dreams. This interest in the exploration of the underlying symbolism of a person's dreams and the ability to communicate through subconscious passageways resulted in a unique, lingering connection to Buchta even after he departed the earth's mortal plane.

A few years prior to Buchta's passing, the author of this biography purchased a used, shiny and white, two-door, two-seat Mercedes sports car convertible that was several model years old. Shortly after licensing the car, he drove it to the home of the Buchta brothers in Lohman since Roger tended to appreciate all things related to Germany, including the products of the country's automotive industry. During the visit, Roger animatedly expressed his adoration for the vehicle. On later occasions, Buchta frequently mentioned the sports car and made remarks about how much he appreciated the vehicle's sleek appearance and style.

"I recently had a dream," explained Sharon Easter, long-time friend and professional colleague of Buchta. "In it, I was standing outside the post office in downtown Russellville, and there was a white car that was making circles around the flagpole. (The flagpole still stands downtown, where it was erected several decades ago.) It was a small, almost glowing-white convertible with two seats and two doors." (Easter never knew about the white sports car once owned by the author.) She continued, "The car then pulled around in front of me, and Roger was driving, grinning from ear to ear. All of a sudden, he took off down the street toward the old school like he was going at warp speed in one of those old sci-fi movies."

With a pause of relief, she added, "There was absolutely nothing frightening about the dream and when I woke up, I was completely at peace. I realized that it was Roger telling me that he was happy and in a good place."

-End-

Roger Dean Buchta

October 28, 1944 – February 5, 2019

APPENDIX A

Below is the radiogram that Private Buchta was able to send to his parents through the Military Affiliate Radio System advising of his safe arrival in Vietnam.

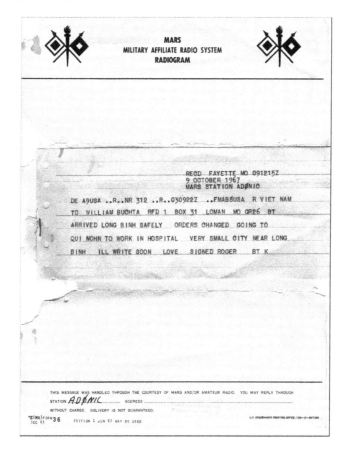

APPENDIX B

In late 1967, Buchta served at Cu Chi, which was just south of the area known as the "Iron Triangle" and west of Saigon (now Ho Chi Minh City).

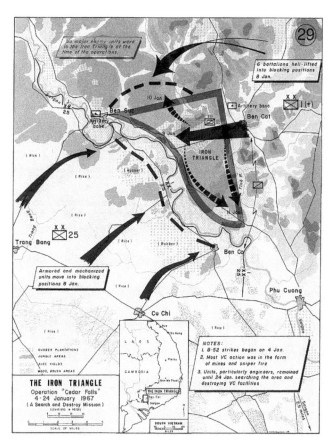

APPENDIX C

While serving in Lai Khe, Vietnam as a medic working with the 18th Surgical Hospital, Roger Buchta received this bulletin when attending a Protestant worship service on January 28 1968, honoring the anniversary of the Army Medical Service.

ARMY MEDICAL SERVICE
ANNIVERSARY

"Come and let us return unto the Lord:
for He hath torn, and He will heal us;
He hath smitten, and He will bind us up."
Hosea 6:1

APPENDIX D

THE 46TH JOHN FINDLEY GREEN LECTURE
at
WESTMINSTER COLLEGE
Fulton, Missouri

Wednesday, May 6, 1992   3:00 p.m.

PROGRAM

Processional   The Skulls of Seven

Invocation   Dr. William A. Young
                                                        Chaplain of the College

The National Anthem   399th U.S. Army Band
                                                         Ft. Leonard Wood, Mo.

Welcome   Dr. J. Harvey Saunders
                                                        President of the College

Greetings   The Honorable John Ashcroft
                                                        Governor of Missouri

Presentation of the Candidate   Yanina Chernenko
for the Honorary Degree of Doctor of Laws   *Westminster College Student*
                                                         St. Petersburg, Russia

Conferral of the Degree   President Saunders
                                                      Dean Richard E. Mattingly

The Lecture   *"The River of Time and the Imperative of Action"*   Mikhail Gorbachev
                                                              Former President
                                              Union of Soviet Socialist Republics

Benediction   Christine Bratkowski
                                                         Student Body President

Recessional

Mr. Gorbachev's trip to the United States is hosted by the Gorbachev Foundation, U.S.A., of San Francisco, CA.

WORKS CITED

Newspapers

Arizona Republic (Phoenix, Arizona)

Asbury Park Press (Asbury, New Jersey)

Bridgeport Post (Bridgeport, Connecticut)

Boonville Daily News, (Boonville, Missouri)

Daily Journal (Vineland, New Jersey)

Gazette (Colorado Springs, Colorado)

Herald-News (Passaic, New Jersey)

Honolulu Advertiser (Honolulu, Hawaii)

Jefferson City Post-Tribune (Jefferson City, Missouri)

Journal News (White Plains, New York)

Los Angeles Times

Moberly Monitor-Index (Moberly, Missouri)

Navajo Times

New York Times

Post and Courier (Charleston, South Carolina)

Spokesman-Review (Spokane, Washington)

Stars and Stripes

St. Joseph News-Press (St. Joseph, Missouri)

Sunday News and Tribune (Jefferson City, Missouri)

Town Talk (Alexandria, Louisiana)

Tribune (Scranton, Pennsylvania)

Washington Post

Books and Articles

Beadle, Christine & Stephen L. Hoffman. "History of Malaria in the United States Naval Forces at War: World War I through the Vietnam Conflict." *Clinical Infectious Diseases* 16, No. 2 (February 1993): 320-329. https://www.jstor.org/stable/4456917?seq=1.

Brimelow, Ben. *50 years ago, US troops bunkered down for the Vietnam War's most infamous siege—here's how the Battle of Khe Shan unfolded.* Business Insider, January 26, 2018. Accessed April 22, 2020. https://www.businessinsider.com/vietnam-war-battle-of-khe-sanh-us-2018-1.

Burowiec, Steven. *Allegations of S. Korean atrocities arising 40 years after Vietnam War.* The Los Angeles Times, May 16, 2015. Accessed April 10, 2020. https://www.latimes.com/world/asia/la-fg-korea-vietnam-20150516-story.html.

Goodwin, Thelma P. (Ed.). *State of Missouri Official Manual: 1965-1966.* Jefferson City, MO: Von Hoffman Press, Inc., 1966.

Headquarters, 18th Surgical Hospital (MA). *Operational Report for Quarterly Period Ending 31 July 1966, Reports Control Symbol CSFOR-65.* Department of the Army: August 15, 1966. Accessed April 24, 2020. https://apps.dtic.mil/dtic/tr/fulltext/u2/874138.pdf.

Herring, George C. *America's Longest War: The United States and Vietnam, 1950-1975 (Second Edition)*. New York, NY: Newberry Awards, Inc., 1986.

Karnow, Stanley. *Vietnam: A History*. New York: The Viking Press, 1983.

Millner, Gloria. *The Tet Offensive*. The Plain Dealer (January 25, 2008). https://www.cleveland.com/pdopinion/2008/01/the_tet_offensive.html (accessed April 22, 2020).

Powell, Alvin. "How Sputnik Changed U.S. Education." The Harvard Gazette (October 11, 2007). https://news.harvard.edu/gazette/story/2007/10/how-sputnik-changed-u-s-education/ (accessed March 25, 2009).

Raithel, Erna E. (Editor). *Russellville, Mo. Sesquicentennial: 1838-1988*. Versailles, MO: B-W Graphics, Inc., 1988.

Sheehan, Neil. *A Bright Shining Lie: John Paul Vann and America in Vietnam*. New York: Random House, 1988.

Taylor, Frederick. *The Berlin Wall: A World Divided, 1961-1989*. New York: HarperCollins Publishers, 2004.

Trass, Adrian G. *The U.S. Army Campaigns of the Vietnam War: Turing Point, 1967-1968 (CMH Pub 76-5)*. Washington, D.C.: Center of Military History, United States Army, 2017.

Tucker, Spencer C. (Editor). *Encyclopedia of the Vietnam War: A Political, Social and Military History*. Santa Barbara, CA: ABC-CLIO, LLC, 2011.

University of Minnesota. "US, UK, Canada to jointly test plague vaccines." Center for Infectious Disease Research and Policy, April 21, 2005. https://www.cidrap.umn.edu/news-perspective/2005/04/us-uk-canada-jointly-test-plague-vaccines (accessed April 30, 2020).

U.S. Army Medical Department, Office of Medical History. *Medical Support of the U.S. Army in the Vietnam War*. Washington, DC: Department of the Army, 1991.

Welsh, Douglas. *The History of the Vietnam War*. New York: Galahad Books, 1981.

Online Resources

Air Mobility Command Museum. *Airlift During the Vietnam War*. Accessed October 3, 2020. https://amcmuseum.org/history/airlift-during-the-vietnam-war/.

Armed Forces Vietnam Network Memories. *KLIK—The "Big Red One."* Accessed April 22, 2020. https://www.afvnvets.net/klik--1st-inf-div..html.

BoxRec. *Floyd Patterson vs. Jerry Quarry (2nd Meeting)*. Accessed April 10, 2020. https://boxrec.com/media/index.php/Floyd_Patterson_vs._Jerry_Quarry_(2nd_meeting).

Connolly, Kate. "Whatever Happened to the Berlin Wall?," *The Guardian,* November 4, 2019, https://www.theguardian.com/news/2019/nov/04/whatever-happened-to-the-berlin-wall.

Department of Defense Financial Management Regulation. *DOD 7000.14-R, Volume 7A, Chapter 51 "Savings Deposit Program (SDP)*, February 2002. Accessed May 18, 2020. https://comptroller.defense.gov/Portals/45/documents/fmr/archive/07aarch/07a_51.pdf.

First Infantry Division Museum at Cantigny. *History of the First Infantry Division: Vietnam*. Accessed June 8, 2020. https://www.fdmuseum.org/about-the-1st-infantry-division/his-

tory-of-the-first-division/#:~:text=The%20Division%20
made%20innovative%20use,general%20would%20be%20
a%20casualty.

French, Patrick. "M-14 Rifle." *National Museum of the U.S Army.*
Accessed March 25, 2020. https://armyhistory.org/m14-rifle/.

GlobalSecurity.org. *47th Brigade Support Battalion.* Accessed March 25,
2020. https://www.globalsecurity.org/military/agency/army/
47fsb.htm

Greater Killeen Chamber of Commerce. *History of Fort Hood.*
Accessed March 24, 2020. https://killeenchamber.com/history
offorthood.

Green Cross International. Mikhail Gorbachev. Accessed May 4,
2020. https://www.gcint.org/who-we-are/our-people/mikhail-
gorbachev/.

History. *Berlin is Divided.* Accessed March 10, 2020. https://www.
history.com/this-day-in-history/berlin-is-divided.

Military Working Dog Team Support Association. *German Shepherd
Dogs in the Military: A Brief Historical Overview.* Accessed
April 23, 2020. https://www.mwdtsa.org/german-shepherd-
dogs-military-brief-historical-overview/

National Archives and Records Administration. *Vietnam War
U.S. Military Casualty Statistics.* Accessed April 28, 2020.
https://www.archives.gov/research/military/vietnam-war/
casualty-statistics#category.

National Churchill Museum. *Mikhail Gorbachev 5/6/92: The Closing
of an Era.* Accessed May 10, 2020. https://www.nationalchur-
chillmuseum.org/mikhail-gorbachev-green-lecture.html

National Park Service. *Civil Rights Act of 1964.* Accessed March 25,
2020. https://www.nps.gov/articles/civil-rights-act.htm.

Naval History and Heritage Command. *Pueblo (AGER-2)*. Accessed April 22, 2020. https://www.history.navy.mil/browse-by-topic/ships/modern-ships/pueblo.html.

Nobel Prize. *Mikhail Gorbachev: Facts*. Accessed May 4, 2020. https://www.nobelprize.org/prizes/peace/1990/gorbachev/facts/

Nobel Prize. Ernest Miller Hemingway. Accessed June 2, 2020. https://www.nobelprize.org/prizes/literature/1954/summary/

Ohio History Connection. *What do you know about C-Rations?* Accessed April 23, 2020. https://www.ohiohistory.org/learn/collections/history/history-blog/2015/july/typecrations.

Selective Service System. *Induction Statistics*. Accessed March 24, 2020. https://www.sss.gov/history-and-records/induction-statistics/

Tour of Duty Advisor. *R&R and Leave in Vietnam*. Accessed April 23, 2020. https://tourofdutyinfol.com

United States Army Center of Military History. *Lineage and Honors: 542nd Medical Company*. Accessed April 11, 2020. https://history.army.mil/html/forcestruc/lineages/branches/med/0542m-dco.htm?fbclid=IwAR13QTNJAcn2M2k05cUBuBDm-Vlq0y_bqTpvK9ZrkZLfT4x8fmk5JcmBodhI.

United States Department of State, Office of the Historian. *The Cuban Missile Crisis, October 1962*. Accessed March 12, 2020. https://history.state.gov/milestones/1961-1968/cuban-missile-crisis.

The White House. *Richard M. Nixon*. Accessed May 1, 2020. https://www.whitehouse.gov/about-the-white-house/presidents/richard-m-nixon/

United States Department of State, Office of the Historian. U.S. Involvement in the Vietnam War: The Tet Offensive, 1968. Accessed April 20, 2020. https://history.state.gov/milestones/1961-1968/tet.

Vergun, David. *Army's Military Radio Auxiliary System still relevant in Internet age.* The website of the U.S. Army (December 17, 2013). Accessed March 30, 2020. https://www.army.mil/article/117034/armys_military_auxiliary_radio_system_still_relevant_in_internet_age.

Vietnam War Travel. *Lai Khe Base Camp.* Accessed April 10, 2020. https://namwartravel.com/lai-khe-base-camp/.

Vietnam War Travel. *DMZ Quang Tri.* Accessed April 22, 2020. https://namwartravel.com/quang-tri/

Visit Berlin. *Checkpoint Charlie: The Scene of Espionage Thrillers.* Accessed June 4, 2020. https://www.visitberlin.de/en/checkpoint-charlie.

Wissing, Doug. *The Return of ROTC.* The American Legion Magazine (December 20, 2012). Accessed March 22, 2020. https://www.legion.org/magazine/213230/return-rotc.

INDEX

Bishop, Joey 84

Boice, Jerry 33-34, 41, 49, 107-109

Bond, Miriam 15

Buchta, Alma 1-2, 5, 9, 220, 239

Buchta, Don vii, xii-xiii, 1-4, 8-10, 13, 16, 30, 32, 37, 39, 47, 53, 60, 63, 67, 76, 81, 86, 93, 98, 104, 112, 115, 120, 124-125, 130, 138, 143, 147-148, 158, 161, 166, 171, 178, 185, 193, 196-198, 201, 207, 210-212, 216, 219-221, 226, 238, 240-241, 246-247.

Buchta, John Jacob 3-4

Buchta, William 1,2, 4, 226, 230

Carman, Gale 33-34, 49, 107-109, 122

Carson, Johnny 84-85

Dunn, Steve 27-28

Easter, Sharon 223, 235, 240, 251

Eberhart, Dr. E.M. 2-3

Engelbrecht, Curtis 13

Engelbrecht, Frances 12-13, 219, 223

Frisby, Charles 191-192

Frisby, Dana 191-194

Gorbachev, Pres. Mikhail 237-239

Hall, Alan 25, 33-34, 49, 107-108

Heidbreder, Marvin 7, 8, 18

Hemingway, Ernest 87-88

Hood, Gen. John Bell 23

Hope, Bob 60, 83, 96-98

Jobe, Joe 234-236

Johnson, Pres. Lyndon   19, 58, 71, 113, 120, 174, 183

Jones, Jane   9-11

Kasike, Kay   231-232

Kennedy, Pres. John F.   17

King Jr., Martin Luther   178

Koestner, John F.   9

Koestner, Rudolph   9

Kruse, Terry   140-141

Linsenbardt, Don   35

McKee, Paul   140

Nixon, Pres. Richard   218

Noel, Chris   83

Patterson, Floyd   57, 59, 63

Quarry, Jerry   57, 59, 63

Russell, David   227-230

Russell, Maribeth   228-229

Snead, Grover   140, 220, 225

Stubinger, Craig   233

Stubinger, Donita   232

Thompson, Ben   230-231

Thompson, Jana   229-230

Verbeck, Dwight   199, 207

Ware, Maj. Gen. Keith L.   125

Welch, Raquel   97-98

Westmoreland, Gen. William C.   62, 180, 183

Weyand, Gen. Fred C.   74

Wyss, Nancy   141

CPSIA information can be obtained
at www.ICGtesting.com
Printed in the USA
FSHW021958270321
79885FS